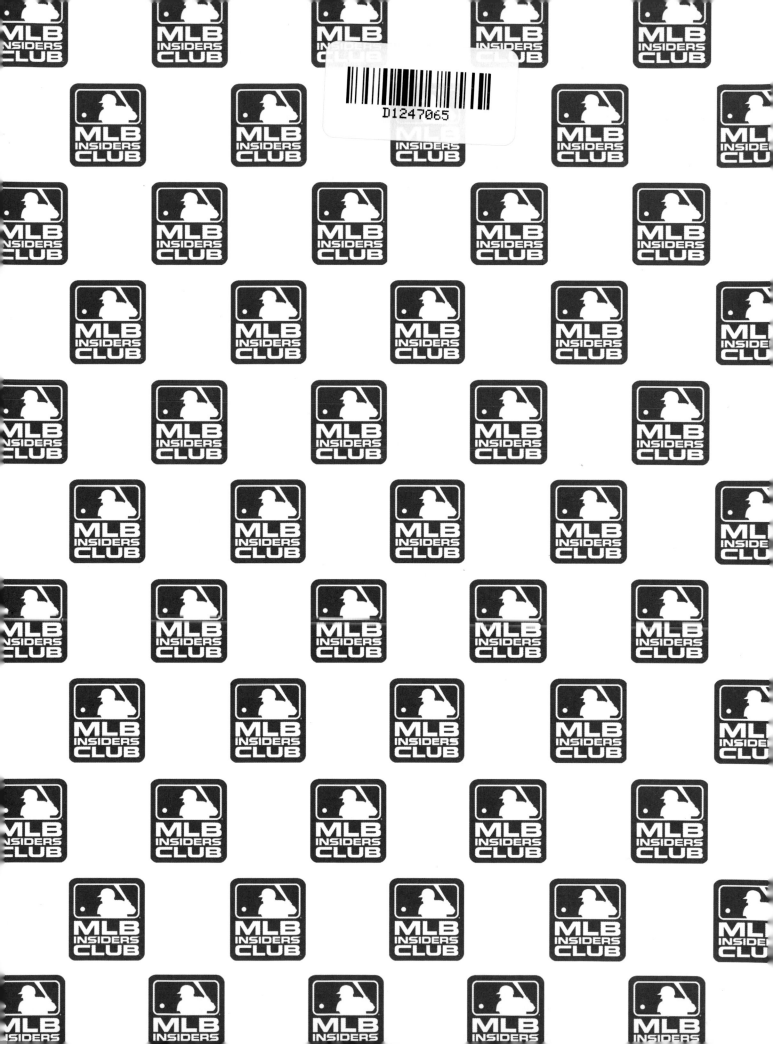

BASEBALL'S
GREATEST
ROOKIES

First-year phenoms, can't-miss prospects and unforgettable debut seasons.

Baseball Insiders Library™

BASEBALL'S
GREATEST
ROOKIES

First-year phenoms, can't-miss prospects and unforgettable debut seasons.

BASEBALL'S GREATEST ROOKIES by Pete Williams

First-year phenoms, can't-miss prospects and unforgettable debut seasons.

Printed in 2011

About the Author

Pete Williams has covered Major League Baseball for nearly two decades for numerous media outlets, including USA Today, The New York Times, SportsBusiness Journal *and* Fox Sports. *The author or co-author of 12 books, including* Inside the World Series *and* Inside Spring Training *in the* Baseball Insiders Library™, *he lives with his wife and two sons in Safety Harbor, Fla.*

Acknowledgements

Major League Baseball would like to thank Pat Kelly and Milo Stewart Jr. at the National Baseball Hall of Fame and Museum for their invaluable assistance; as well as Eric Enders, Bill Francis, Nathan Hale and Kristin Nieto for their diligent work in helping to prepare the book for publication.

Major League Baseball Properties

Vice President, Publishing
Donald S. Hintze

Editorial Director
Mike McCormick

Publications Art Director
Faith M. Rittenberg

Senior Production Manager
Claire Walsh

Associate Editor
Jon Schwartz

Associate Art Director
Melanie Finnern

Senior Publishing Coordinator
Anamika Chakrabarty

Project Assistant Editors
Chris Greenberg, Jodie Jordan,
Jake Schwartzstein

Editorial Intern
Allison Duffy

Major League Baseball Photos

Director
Rich Pilling

Photo Editor
Jessica Foster

MLB Insiders Club

Creative Director
Tom Carpenter

Managing Editor
Jen Weaverling

Prepress
Wendy Holdman

3 4 5 6 7 8 9 10 / 12 11

Copyright © MLB Insiders Club 2009

ISBN: 978-1-58159-440-9

MLB Insiders Club
12301 Whitewater Drive
Minnetonka, MN 55343

TABLE OF CONTENTS

Introduction		6
Chapter 1	Signs of Things To Come	8
Chapter 2	Flash in the Pan	20
Chapter 3	Teenagers	30
Chapter 4	Better Late Than Never	40
Chapter 5	Land of the Rising Stars	48
Chapter 6	Charisma	56
Chapter 7	Blasting Onto the Scene	66
Chapter 8	Mound Presence	76
Chapter 9	Fast Track	82
Chapter 10	Cooperstown Bound	94
Chapter 11	Best Prospects Ever	104
Chapter 12	No. 1 Picks	116
Chapter 13	Seamless Transition	124
Chapter 14	Late-Season Call-Ups	136
Chapter 15	World Series Rookies	144
Source Notes/Credits		156
Index		158

During his Hall of Fame induction speech in 1989, Red Sox legend Carl Yastrzemski — the last player to win the Triple Crown — looked back over his 23-year career and remarked, "I remember in 1961 when I was a scared rookie, hitting .220 after the first three months of my baseball season, doubting my ability."

Even years after his rookie campaign, as he was enshrined amongst the game's all-time greats, the feeling of insecurity from his debut season still clung to him like pine tar. Carrying a .247 batting average into the 1961 All-Star break, Yastrzemski was a scuffling 21-year-old; Cooperstown might as well have been a city on Jupiter.

Thanks in part to the combination of potential and vulnerability in young ballplayers, few things capture the attention of a sports fan more quickly than the emergence of a promising rookie. Whether a touted prospect or a player that bursts onto the scene from obscurity, a rookie can energize a team and its fan base. From Ty Cobb and Walter Johnson to Joe DiMaggio and Willie Mays to Albert Pujols and Chipper Jones, many of baseball's all-time greats, not surprisingly, enjoyed stellar freshman campaigns.

Baseball has an uncanny ability to produce charismatic rookie players, often pitchers, who mesmerize fans with their dynamic personalities and eccentricities on the field. Mark "The Bird" Fidrych

became a national sensation for the Tigers in 1976, although no more so than the Dodgers' Fernando Valenzuela, who won the Cy Young Award and a World Series ring as a rookie in 1981, and who triggered "Fernandomania" throughout Los Angeles.

Some players, like Cobb, Bob Feller and Robin Yount, made major impacts as teenagers. Players such as Al Kaline, Dave Winfield and Bob Horner took the express route to the Majors, not playing a day in the Minors. Others, such as Elston Howard and Hoyt Wilhelm, were late bloomers. And then there was Jim Morris, the 35-year-old whose unlikely stint with the Tampa Bay Devil Rays in 1999 became the basis for the movie *The Rookie*.

Guys like Tom Seaver and Fred Lynn, Derek Jeter and Evan Longoria, managed to make the game look easy from day one. Then there are those rookies so poised that they star on baseball's grandest stage. From Pepper Martin and Whitey Ford to Livan Hernandez, Francisco Rodriguez and Dustin Pedroia, several rookies have delivered key performances during the World Series.

Baseball is the only major team sport that mirrors the calendar. Each year provides a new generation of stars to replace the old, with each rookie emerging on his own timeline. The following narratives show us another side of many players, catching them at a time when they still had to prove themselves.

chapter 1

SIGNS OF THINGS TO COME

For some players, there is no learning curve, no indoctrination period needed. From day one of their rookie seasons, they look like seasoned veterans, making a difficult game appear easy. More impressively, they translate that early success into long, distinguished careers. Remarkably, these players tend to be unheralded, like 62nd-round draft pick Mike Piazza, lanky Jeff Bagwell or Ramon Martinez's kid brother, Pedro. Even Albert Pujols, perhaps the greatest hitter of his generation, arrived to little fanfare in 2001. Years later, we look back on these promising early days as merely a sign of great things to come.

ALBERT PUJOLS 2001

In 2001, Albert Pujols reported to Cardinals Spring Training camp in Jupiter, Fla., as a non-roster player with just one year of pro experience, all but three games of it at the Single-A level.

Over the winter, St. Louis had traded third baseman Fernando Tatis to Montreal, in part because Pujols hit .314 with 19 homers and 96 RBI in the Minors. They thought he might be ready to assume the job full time as early as 2002.

In camp, Manager Tony La Russa asked Pujols, then a third baseman, to play the outfield, where he made some fine plays. When La Russa gave Pujols a day off, he took grounders at short-stop. Impressed, La Russa put Pujols at short the next day, where he started a double play on the first ball hit to him. Before breaking camp, La Russa told Pujols that he made the team.

"But he told me it might just be for the (first) series in Colorado," Pujols said. "He didn't know if I would stay after that."

HR	RBI	AVG	SLG
37	130	.329	.610

Bobby Bonilla's hamstring injury opened a spot for Pujols, 21, at third. In the second series of the season, against Arizona, the rookie hit a home run and three doubles, driving in eight runs. In May, he was named NL Rookie of the Month. He became the first Cardinals rookie to be named to the All-Star Game since 1955.

A virtual unknown at the start of 2001, Pujols wasn't even drafted in many fantasy leagues. By season's end, his year was being mentioned among the best ever by a rookie. He batted .329 with an NL rookie–record 130 RBI. He led the Cardinals in average, homers (37), RBI, hits (194) and doubles (47) while playing 39 or more games each at first and third base, and in both left and right field.

"It doesn't matter where I play," Pujols said in 2001, upon learning of his Rookie of the Year honor. "I'm just going to Spring Training and trying to make the team again."

9

JOE JACKSON 1911

Joe Jackson's beautiful left-handed hitting stroke, one Babe Ruth would later emulate, was evident by the age of 13. Too young to work in the local mill in rural South Carolina, Jackson was allowed to play for the Brandon Mill baseball team.

It was there that he reportedly removed a pair of ill-fitting new cleats and played the rest of the game in his stocking feet. When he hit a home run, a fan of the other team shouted, "Oh, you shoeless son of a bitch." Scoop Latimer, a reporter for *The Greensville News*, censored the comment and shortened the nickname to "Shoeless Joe."

Jackson began his professional career in 1908 when Connie Mack signed him to play for the Philadelphia Athletics. Jackson was up and down between the Major and Minor Leagues during his first two seasons, playing just 10 games with the A's. Dealt to the Cleveland Naps (later the Indians) before the 1910 season, he hit .387 (29 for 75) in 20 games.

HR	RBI	AVG	H
7	83	.408	233

In 1911, he went up to the Big Leagues for good, batting .408 and leading the American League with a .468 on-base percentage. His .408 batting average, a Major League rookie record that still stands, was only good for a distant second-place showing in the AL batting race, as Ty Cobb hit .420.

He batted .395 in his sophomore outing, leading the AL in triples (26) and tying Cobb for the most hits (226). Once again, he finished second in batting to Cobb, who hit .409. Jackson would hit at a .357 clip over 10 full seasons before receiving a lifetime ban from the sport because of his connection with the Black Sox scandal in the 1919 World Series.

"I hit .408 and I hit .395, and I still don't win the batting title," Jackson said, in his Southern drawl, of his first two years. "This is a mighty tough league."

Jackson would hit at a .357 clip over 10 full seasons before receiving a lifetime ban from the sport because of his connection with the Black Sox scandal in the 1919 World Series.

JEFF BAGWELL 1991

Entering the 1991 season, the Astros didn't expect much from the scrawny infielder acquired via trade the previous August. But by the end of the year, sportswriters were calling the trade for Jeff Bagwell one of the best moves ever, and were applauding Astros Assistant GM Bob Watson, who had scouted the former Red Sox prospect before the trade.

HR	RBI	AVG	H
15	82	.294	163

"I watched him hit rising line drives to center and right-center," Watson said. "He reminded me of Don Mattingly, the way he comes out of that crouch when he swings."

Having played no position but third, where Ken Caminiti was entrenched, the 22-year-old had no clear role when he reported to spring camp. But Bagwell saw an opening when it became clear that Mike Simms was not ready to play first. He never looked back, becoming a Rookie of the Year contender. When a slump dropped his average to .280, teammate Casey Candaele lit a fire under him, saying, "I remember when Jeff Bagwell was in the running for Rookie of the Year."

Bagwell ended strong, hitting .325 in September and October and leading the team in homers and RBI. He fell one vote shy of a unanimous Rookie of the Year win.

"Once I started looking at everything," Bagwell said, "I would have been disappointed if I hadn't won."

DICK ALLEN 1964

VADA PINSON 1959

Dick Allen's professional baseball career got off to a rocky start. He endured racism in Little Rock, Ark., where he became the first African-American to suit up for the Philadelphia Phillies' Minor League affiliate. Although he faced similar abuse later from some fans in Philadelphia, Allen didn't let anyone keep him from having an incredible rookie season in 1964. He led the Phillies to pennant contention by batting .318 with 29 home runs and 91 RBI, leading the NL in runs scored (125), triples (13) and total bases (352).

HR	RBI	AVG	SLG
29	91	.318	.557

Mistakenly referred to as "Richie" during his first stint in Philadelphia, the Pennsylvania native wielded a 42-ounce bat and a brash personality while smacking Ruthian homers. When he won the NL Rookie of the Year Award, Phillies Manager Gene Mauch called him a sure bet for the Triple Crown during his career. Indeed, with the White Sox in '72, Allen fell short solely in average, coming within 10 points of the title.

Every year, there are players who think they should have won the Rookie of the Year Award but didn't — Vada Pinson might have the best case. With 96 at-bats during two trips to the Bigs in '58, he was disqualified from rookie status in 1959 by just six at-bats.

A lean 5 foot 11 and 175 pounds, the 20-year-old played in all 154 games for the Reds in '59, dominating with a smooth, compact, lefty swing. He led the NL in runs (131), doubles (47) and at-bats (648), and finished second in hits (205) and

HR	RBI	AVG	H
20	84	.316	205

fourth in batting (.316). Although Reds Manager Fred Hutchinson noted Pinson had yet to learn how to get a good jump on pitchers, he stole 21 bases, fifth-most in the NL, while showing flashes of the defense in center field that would earn him a Gold Glove Award two years later. "That Vada," said teammate Frank Robinson, "is making a joke out of this game." Ineligible for the Rookie of the Year Award that went to Willie McCovey of the Giants, Pinson finished 15th in NL MVP voting.

SIGNS OF THINGS TO COME

TONY OLIVA 1964

Tony Oliva was not the first or the last Latino to arrive in the Majors with confusion about his identity and age. Signed by the Twins out of Cuba in 1961, the discrepancy arose because one of Oliva's friends told the team that 21-year-old Tony was actually his 18-year-old brother, Pedro. It didn't help that Tony had used Pedro's passport to enter the U.S. The incorrect age continued to appear in newspapers during Oliva's 1964 rookie season, and he was considered 23, not 26.

At any age, Oliva enjoyed a spectacular debut campaign, adding a powerful left-handed bat to the AL's most potent lineup. With a level swing that let him adjust to low and high pitches, Oliva transitioned easily to the Bigs, batting .441 as late as mid-May. For the season, he hit .323, becoming the first player to win both the Rookie of the Year Award and AL batting title. Oliva also led the AL in hits (217), doubles (43), extra-base hits (84), total bases (374) and runs (109) while appearing in the All-Star Game and finishing fourth in the MVP voting.

Teammates raved about his cheerful, quiet disposition, and his mastery of the game despite having limited knowledge of its history. But his hitting was a finished product. "Nobody ever touched his hitting," said Twins scout Del Wilber. "I'd see him around the cage even when he wasn't supposed to hit, and I'd tell him to go out there and field. He knew how to hit."

ROOKIES TO WIN BATTING TITLE		
PLAYER	AVG	YEAR
Pete Browning	.430	1882
Benny Kauff	.370	1914
Tony Oliva	**.323**	1964
Ichiro Suzuki	.350	2001

HR	RBI	AVG	H
32	94	.323	217

PETE BROWNING 1882

The original "Louisville Slugger," for whom the bat company is named, Louis Rogers "Pete" Browning was better known as "the Gladiator" because of his battles with journalists and alcoholism.

Born in Louisville, Ky., in 1861 — the youngest of eight children — Browning was a skilled marbles player and figure skater as a child. From a young age, Browning suffered from a condition that robbed him of most of his hearing. As a result, he shunned school and was functionally illiterate as an adult. The sense of isolation, along with the physical discomfort created by his condition, later contributed to his alcoholism. Neither had much impact on his athletic skills, however.

He made his professional baseball debut on April 13, 1877 — two months shy of his 16th birthday — for the city's well-known semi-pro club, the Eclipse. In July he pitched the Eclipse to a 4-0 victory over the National League's Louisville Grays.

In 1882, the Eclipse went Major League as a charter member of the American Association, the National League's first great rival. The 21-year-old Browning put together one of the greatest rookie seasons ever. He ran away with the league batting title, posting a .378 average that was 36 points better than that of his nearest rival, Hick Carpenter of Cincinnati. It also was the best average in the Majors, 10 points better than Dan Brouthers' NL mark.

Browning also led the American Association in on-base percentage (.430) and slugging (.510), while ranking second in hits (109), fourth in total bases (147) and runs scored (67). He was among the league leaders in home runs (5) and walks (26).

HR	H	AVG	OBP
5	109	.378	.430

SIGNS OF THINGS TO COME

PEDRO MARTINEZ 1993

In 1993, the younger brother of Dodgers ace Ramon Martinez, Pedro, brought a high-90s fastball and a swagger to the L.A. bullpen, even though he carried just 158 pounds on his rail-thin, 5-foot-11 frame.

The young right-hander had dislocated his left shoulder swinging a bat in Triple-A Albuquerque late in the 1992 season. Dr. Frank Jobe, the longtime Dodgers physician, repaired the shoulder however, and Martinez quickly excelled in the set-up role for closer Jim Gott in '93. Martinez made 65 appearances, 63 in relief, and posted a 10-5 record, 2.61 ERA and 119 strikeouts. Even after the promising 1993 performance, there were concerns about Martinez's durability. Unlike Ramon, who at 6 foot 4 looked like a classic starting pitcher, Pedro's slight frame provoked debate in the Dodgers' front office about whether his future was as a starter or reliever.

"He had kind of a delicate stature to start with, and there were already questions about his stamina," Jobe said. "It's a judgment call, but you had to kind of wonder, 'Golly, is this kid going to break down?'"

With a glaring hole at second base, L.A. decided it did not want to wait to see how Martinez developed. On Nov. 19, 1993, GM Fred Claire dealt the ninth-place finisher in the Rookie of the Year balloting to the Expos for Delino DeShields.

Before starting the 1999 All-Star Game for the AL, Martinez mentioned the '93 trade as ongoing motivation.

"I made 65 appearances in '93 and they were still saying I was too small, too weak, certain to break down. I think about it all the time. It's my motivation. Durability is my whole game. I've proven them wrong."

W	L	ERA	IP
10	5	2.61	107

MIKE PIAZZA 1993

Mike Piazza got to the Majors the hard way. His journey began in a makeshift batting cage behind his childhood home in the Philadelphia suburbs. A washout at the University of Miami who moved on to Miami Dade Community College, he was selected in the 62nd round of the 1988 draft, the 1,389th pick. The move was a favor — Piazza's father, Vincent, and Dodgers Manager Tommy Lasorda were childhood friends — and seen as nothing more than a way for the first baseman to attract attention from four-year schools.

Instead, Piazza asked for a tryout, impressed Dodgers brass with his hitting, and agreed to become a catcher if that would get him to the Bigs. When L.A. didn't re-sign 13-year-veteran Mike Scioscia after the 1992 season, they entered Spring Training without a catcher. Piazza responded by hitting .478 with four homers in the spring.

Once the season started, Piazza continued to pound the ball like no Dodgers backstop since Roy Campanella. Perhaps it should not have been a surprise. Ted Williams once had watched a teenage Piazza in the backyard batting cage, a visit arranged through Vincent's connections.

"Mike hits it harder than I did when I was 16," Williams said. "I guarantee you this kid will hit the ball."

With more career homers than any catcher, perhaps no backstop ever hit better. As a rookie, Piazza hit .318 with 35 home runs and 112 RBI. He was a unanimous selection for NL Rookie of the Year, the second in a stretch of five Dodgers — including his good buddy Eric Karros the previous season — to capture the award. No player was a more unlikely winner.

HR	RBI	AVG	SLG
35	112	.318	.561

Raines (sliding)

TIM RAINES 1981

When Ron LeFlore signed with the White Sox as a free agent before the 1981 season, the Expos lost their speedy leadoff man. They found a good replacement in 21-year-old Tim Raines. Raines hit .354 with 77 steals and 105 runs in 1980, earning Minor League Player of the Year honors. Although he had not played the outfield regularly since high school, the Expos put him in left field in the spring and batted him leadoff.

So highly regarded was Raines that 18 teams had been interested in him over the winter. The Cubs even dangled Cy Young–winner Bruce Sutter. "If we had yielded to temptation," said Expos

H	AVG	OBP	SB
95	.304	.391	71

President John McHale, "we would have run the risk of repeating the same error the Cubs made when they traded Lou Brock."

Earning the nickname "Rock" because he had just 7.8 percent body fat, Raines was a terror on the basepaths. At the plate, the natural right-hander learned to switch-hit so well that he became better from the left side.

Raines stole 71 bases in the strike-shortened 1981 season, the first of four straight years he led the NL. Were it not for "Fernandomania" sweeping the league in the form of Dodger Fernando Valenzuela, Raines would have been Rookie of the Year.

Garciaparra (in air)

NOMAR GARCIAPARRA 1997

Rarely have Boston fans embraced a player as quickly as they did Nomar Garciaparra in 1997. With his powerful bat, endearing obsessive-compulsive routine at the plate and tireless work ethic, "No-Mah" was an immediate fan favorite.

A gangly shortstop when drafted in 1994, he turned to his former Georgia Tech trainer Mark Verstegen after the '95 season for help developing the rotational strength in his core to uncoil ferocious power with each swing. As a result, Garciaparra hit 30 home runs as a rookie with 98 RBI, setting a record for RBI by a leadoff hitter. He compiled a 30-game hitting streak, competed in

HR	RBI	AVG	H
30	98	.306	209

the Home Run Derby, finished eighth in the AL MVP voting and was a unanimous selection for Rookie of the Year.

Garciaparra earned the nickname "No Nonsense Nomar" in Tee Ball as a 6-year-old, and brought the same intensity to the Bigs. "I don't know anyone more driven," teammate Aaron Sele said.

Garciaparra's start was even more impressive because of the pressure put on him when Boston shortstop John Valentin protested being moved to second. "People felt Nomar began playing under a microscope," Manager Jimy Williams said. "But the first time I saw him, I knew he had the instincts to be a star."

chapter 2

FLASH IN THE PAN

They arrive with such promise, showing the type of unspoiled, awe-inspiring talent that gets managers salivating. Fans begin to envision multiple trips to the All-Star Game during the next decade, perhaps even a Hall of Fame plaque. Then, often just as quickly as these highly touted prospects arrive, they flame out. The phenomenon is known as the "flash in the pan," and it's heartbreakingly common in baseball. Whether due to injuries, pressure or the rest of the league figuring them out, some of baseball's most promising young stars never fulfill their potential, leaving fans to wonder things like, "Where have you gone Joe Charboneau?"

JOE CHARBONEAU 1980

The legend of Joe Charboneau preceded his promotion to the Indians. The easygoing 6-foot-2, 200-pound brute scraped a tattoo off his arm with a razor blade; performed his own oral surgery using a razor blade, pliers and whiskey; earned spare cash as a bare-knuckle fighter; and drank beer through his nose after opening the bottle with his eye socket. The larger-than-life ballplayer owned a pet alligator and survived a stabbing by a pen-wielding lunatic in Mexico.

His Big League debut was no less notice-able.

HR	RBI	AVG	H
23	87	.289	131

He smashed a home run in his second at-bat in the Indians' 1980 opener, on the road against the Angels. By the time the Tribe returned home, Charboneau was a fan favorite, receiving a standing ovation during pregame introductions. He responded by going 3 for 3 with a double and a home run.

A song was written about him and a fan club formed, taking residence in Section 36 of Cleveland Stadium. Sportswriter Terry Pluto of the *Plain Dealer* dubbed him "Super Joe" and wondered if this out-of-nowhere left fielder was Joe Hardy of *Damn Yankees*.

For one year, he was. Despite missing much of the last six weeks of the 1980 season because of an injury suffered running into a railing at Comiskey Park, he hit .289 with 23 home runs. He tallied 87 RBI and won the American League Rookie of the Year Award. The following spring, Charboneau injured his back sliding headfirst. His career spiraled downward from there. He played in just 70 more games through 1982, becoming the embodiment of the phrase "flash in the pan."

"I really wasn't a franchise player," Charboneau told *Sports Illustrated* in 1992. "I wasn't even that good. I couldn't run. I wasn't gonna steal bases or drive in runs. But baseball was dead in Cleveland, and the Indians needed someone to generate some interest in the club, to make baseball fun again."

GEORGE McQUILLAN 1908

George McQuillan enjoyed one of the best rookie seasons in history in 1908. The 23-year-old righty went 23-17 for the fourth-place Phillies with a dazzling 1.53 ERA in nearly 360 innings of work in the midst of the Deadball Era. Considered an unusually fast worker on the hill, even in an era of quick games, McQuillan became known as the sport's most promising young pitcher.

During his sophomore campaign, McQuillan won 13 games for the Phillies, another 13 for the Pirates in 1914 and 12 between the two

W	L	ERA	IP
23	17	1.53	359.2

teams the following season. He managed just an 85-89 record over a 10-year career marred by alcoholism, financial problems and a wild personal life. So unreliable was McQuillan because of alcohol and a lack of conditioning that the Phillies parted with him after the 1910 season even though he posted a league-leading 1.60 ERA.

After pitching for Cleveland in 1918, McQuillan's Big League career was over at age 33. He remained in the Minors until 1924.

Russell (center)

REB RUSSELL 1913

A Texas farm boy who grew up throwing mostly curveballs, Ewell Albert "Reb" Russell was forced to rely on his fastball and change-up after he took a line drive off his thumb in 1912 while pitching in the Texas-Oklahoma League. When the Chicago White Sox signed him following the season, the plan was to send him to the Pacific Coast League. Instead, Russell made the Big League roster and put together one of the finest seasons of the Deadball Era. Again using a full arsenal of pitches, Reb went 22-16 with a sub-2.00 ERA.

W	L	ERA	IP
22	16	1.90	316.2

"That boy has everything," Sox Manager Jimmy Callahan marveled. "He has speed. He has curves. He has control. He has nerve. He has strength. What more could I ask for?"

Russell suffered hip and ankle injuries in an on-field collision in 1914. Thus began a pattern of injuries which, compounded with erratic conditioning, resulted in a dead arm by 1919. He returned as an outfielder with the Pirates in 1922, hitting .368 with 12 homers and 75 RBI in 60 games, but never fulfilled his promise.

Black (pitching)

JOE BLACK 1952

Joe Black was 28 years old when he joined the Brooklyn Dodgers in 1952, having already led the Negro Leagues' Baltimore Elite Giants to one title in eight years. Black had all but given up on the Majors until Branch Rickey signed Jackie Robinson.

"When Rickey signed Jackie, I was 18 all over again," Black said years later. "I started dreaming. And that's what happened to most of the guys in the Negro Leagues. You forgot your age. You said, 'If Jackie makes it, I can make it.'"

With a high-octane fastball, the burly 6-foot-2 right-hander quickly emerged as the anchor of the Brooklyn bullpen, posting a 15-4 record with 15 saves and a 2.15 ERA in 56 appearances. He received 19 of 24 first-place votes for NL Rookie of the Year, besting Hoyt Wilhelm, Dick Groat and Eddie Mathews.

Although Black started just two games during the season, Dodgers Manager Charlie Dressen handed him the ball for Game 1 of the World Series against the Yankees at Ebbets Field. Black outdueled Yankees ace Allie Reynolds, pitching a complete-game six-hitter. For the Series, he allowed just six runs in 21.1 innings.

The following spring, Dressen encouraged Black to add more pitches to his repertoire, which then consisted of a fastball and a curve. Sadly, the tinkering caused Black to lose control of those basic pitches.

Black spent three more seasons with Brooklyn and pitched briefly for Cincinnati and Washington. By 1958, he was out of baseball completely, but not before he compiled a 30-12 record in six Big League seasons. Half of his wins came in that magical rookie year.

W	L	ERA	SV
15	4	2.15	15

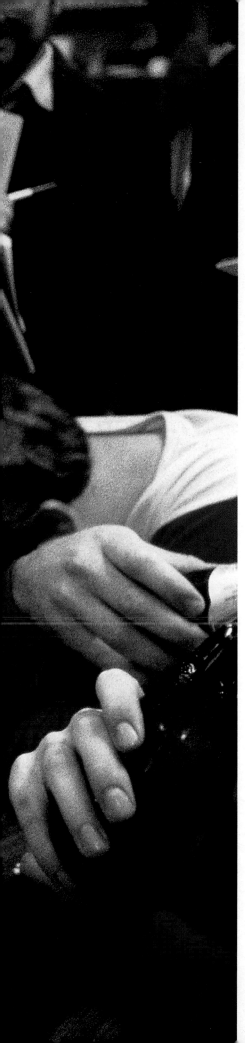

JOHN STUPER 1982

As an eccentric rookie in 1982, John Stuper was known for hamming it up in the club-house as the host of the "John Cosell Show," interviewing his Cardinals teammates by using a beer bottle as a microphone. When he wasn't practicing for a second career in broadcasting, Stuper fared pretty well on the mound. In 23 games (21 starts), he posted a 9-7 record with a 3.36 ERA, becoming a key contributor for the NL East champions.

Despite solid outings, Stuper took no decisions in Game 2 of both the NLCS against the Atlanta Braves and the World Series against the Milwaukee Brewers — games St. Louis won in late innings with closer Bruce Sutter on the mound. But in Game 6 of the Fall Classic, Stuper put together one of baseball's most memorable postseason pitching performances.

The Brewers held a 3-games-to-2 advantage as the Series came back to St. Louis for Game 6 on Oct. 19, 1982. When Stuper threw his first pitch, the temperature was 70 degrees. When the game ended five hours and two rain delays later, the thermometer

W	L	ERA	IP
9	7	3.36	136.2

showed 40 degrees. Stuper, remarkably, went the distance, even after a delay of more than two hours in the bottom of the sixth inning. He returned to pitch the seventh with a 13-0 lead, having allowed just two singles. Afterward, he admitted he had second thoughts about his continued participation in the game.

"There's a fine line between being a hero and being dumb," he said. "I didn't want to go out there and give up three or four quick runs."

He gave up just one, in the ninth inning, in the Cardinals' 13-1 win. Because of the delays, he held a shutout for nearly five hours.

Stuper won 12 games in 1983, but played just two more seasons before an arm injury derailed his career at the age of 28. Rather than try his hand at broadcasting after hanging up his spikes, Stuper became a successful baseball coach at Yale University.

STUPER'S 1982 POSTSEASON STATS						
W	L	CG	ERA	IP	K	BB
1	0	1	3.32	19	9	6

SAM JETHROE 1950

Sam Jethroe could have been the player to break baseball's color barrier. In 1945, the Boston Red Sox invited Jethroe, Jackie Robinson and Marvin Williams to Fenway Park for a tryout. The event was a sham, though, staged to appease a city councilman.

Jethroe, the most accomplished of the trio, was a speedy center fielder for the Cleveland Buckeyes of the Negro American League when Branch Rickey purchased his contract in 1948. The next season, Jethroe stole 89 bases for a Dodgers farm team.

HR	RBI	AVG	SB
18	58	.273	35

"When he came to bat, the infield would have to come in a few steps or you'd never throw him out," said Hall of Famer Buck O'Neil.

Prior to the 1950 season, Rickey sold Jethroe to the Boston Braves. At 32, he batted .273 with 18 homers, 58 RBI and a league-high 35 steals to become the oldest Rookie of the Year. Jethroe played just two more full seasons, finishing with a brief stint with the Pirates in 1954.

GENE BEARDEN 1948

The 1948 Cleveland Indians pitching staff included future Hall of Famers Bob Feller, Bob Lemon and Satchel Paige. But their most reliable starter was actually rookie Gene Bearden. The lefty baffled AL hitters with an assortment of junk pitches. Hall of Famer Ted Williams wrote in *My Turn at Bat* that "every ball [Bearden] threw was either a little knuckleball or a little knuckle-curve."

Bearden went 20-7 with a league-leading 2.43 ERA, with six shutouts. But he saved his best for last. Starting on just

W	L	ERA	IP
20	7	2.43	229.2

one day of rest, he notched his 20th win in a one-game playoff for the pennant against the Red Sox. In Game 3 of the World Series he shut out the Boston Braves, and in Game 6 he relieved Lemon and recorded the final five outs to clinch the title.

Only one Rookie of the Year Award was given at the time, and it went to Alvin Dark of the Braves. Sadly, Bearden couldn't duplicate his rookie season. He never again won more than eight games in a season and twice led the AL in wild pitches.

LOUIS SOCKALEXIS 1897

A member of the Penobscot tribe from Maine and a baseball legend in college at Holy Cross and Notre Dame, Louis Sockalexis jumped directly from the collegiate ranks to the Major Leagues in 1897, becoming the first Native American to play in the Majors and the first minority athlete to play in the National League.

Known by fans as the "Deerfoot of the Diamond" and the "Chief of Sockem," Sockalexis boasted a powerful throwing arm and batted .338 with three home runs, 42 RBI and 16 steals as a rookie for the Cleveland Spiders. But he found the transition to the Major Leagues difficult, enduring ridicule and hatred from sportswriters and fans in other cities.

Like Jackie Robinson 50 years later, Sockalexis tried to ignore the taunts and jeers and aimed to prove doubters wrong with his play on the field. But he acknowledged his detractors in a revealing, rare interview with Cleveland's *Plain Dealer.* "No matter where we play I go through the same ordeal, and at the present time I am so used to it that at times I forget to smile at my tormentors."

Sockalexis, whose problems with alcohol had started in college, was suspended by the Spiders for playing while intoxicated. The alcoholism brought his career to a premature end, as he played in just 28 Big League games over the next two seasons, finishing his career in the Minors.

Not long after his death at the age of 42 in 1913, Cleveland's American League team was named the Indians and Chief Wahoo was adopted as the mascot. How much of that decision was to honor Sockalexis has been open to debate.

HR	RBI	AVG	H
3	42	.338	94

HERB SCORE 1955

How good might Herb Score have been? As a rookie in 1955, Score went 16-10 and struck out an AL-leading 245 batters, a rookie record that stood for 29 years, until Dwight Gooden broke it with the Mets. He threw a devastating curve that complemented a fastball believed to be equal to that of teammate Bob Feller, considered the hardest thrower of the era.

"They didn't have a radar gun then to measure speed," teammate Rocky Colavito said of Score's velocity. "But I think he threw 100 miles an hour."

Score, the AL Rookie of the Year in '55, led the league in strikeouts again in '56 with 263. That year, the lefty won 20 games at a younger age (23) than Sandy Koufax did. During Spring Training in 1957, the Boston Red Sox offered to purchase Score for $1 million, a lofty figure at a time when entire franchises sold for $4 million.

"We wouldn't sell him for $2 million," said Indians GM Hank Greenberg.

On May 7, 1957, Score was part of one of the scariest moments in baseball history while facing the Yankees at Cleveland's Municipal Stadium. The second batter to face him, shortstop Gil McDougald, drilled a low pitch right back at him. The ball struck Score in the face, knocking him down and sending blood streaming from his right eye, nose and mouth.

Score missed the rest of the season, most of the next, and was not the same pitcher once he returned. He finished with a 55-46 record in eight seasons before beginning a long career as an Indians broadcaster.

Said Feller: "He would have been probably one of the greatest, if not *the* greatest, left-handed pitchers who ever lived."

W	L	ERA	K
16	10	2.85	245

MITCHELL PAGE 1977

Mitchell Page was supposed to return the Athletics to their early 1970s glory. An outfielder with speed and power who came to Oakland as part of a blockbuster, nine-player trade with the Pirates in Spring Training 1977, he made an immediate impact.

Playing left field and batting third in a lineup stripped of stars and headlined by aging cleanup hitter Dick Allen, who was in his final season, Page homered twice and drove in six runs on April 13 at the Oakland Coliseum. The effort came against the Angels, who had signed A's stars Don Baylor and Joe Rudi the previous winter.

Early on, Page looked capable of replacing some of their output. For the season, he batted .307 with 21

HR	RBI	AVG	H
21	75	.307	154

home runs, 75 RBI and 42 stolen bases. Page ranked among the AL top 10 in steals, slugging, walks and OBP. Although Page was honored by *The Sporting News* as the 1977 Rookie of the Year, the award handed out by the Baseball Writers Association of America went to Baltimore's Eddie Murray.

The A's won 87 games in '76, but just 63 in Page's rookie season. The club would have just two winning season during his seven years in Oakland. Page's struggles seemed to parallel the team's, as he never replicated his rookie season, and finished his Big League career in 1984 at age 32 after a brief stint with the Pirates.

chapter 3

TEENAGERS

Most teenage baseball players find the level of competition in high school, college or the Minor Leagues more than adequate. But there are a few prodigies who are ready for the Major Leagues shortly after high school or, in the case of Hall of Fame pitcher Bob Feller, before collecting a diploma. Some teenagers, like Walter Johnson, Jimmie Foxx and Robin Yount, mature into the game's all-time greats. Others struggle to deal with the early success, never fulfilling the seemingly limitless potential they showed before their 20th birthdays.

TY COBB 1906

It's doubtful that many Big Leaguers had a more tumultuous teenage experience than Ty Cobb. While playing for Augusta (Ga.) in the South Atlantic League in 1905, the 18-year-old learned that his mother had shot his father dead, thinking he was an intruder.

Within days of his father's death, the Detroit Tigers purchased Cobb's contract. Already known for his tempestuous personality, Cobb feuded with Augusta players and executives on the way out the door. If he didn't make it in Detroit, the reputation he was earning may have prevented him from signing anywhere else. Not that it mattered very much to Cobb at the time.

"In my grief," Cobb later said, "going up didn't matter much. It felt like the end of me."

HR	RBI	AVG	H
1	34	.316	113

In his Big League debut on Aug. 30, 1905, wielding a 38-ounce piece of lumber, Cobb doubled off of New York's Jack Chesbro in his first at-bat. His speed and aggressive baserunning were by turns brilliant and reckless, aggravating teammates and the Tigers' small cadre of fans. When the season ended, Cobb had no guarantee of a contract, and not too many friends in the game.

In January, Cobb signed a $1,500 agreement and reported to camp as a fourth outfielder. Hazed by veteran teammates who no doubt felt threatened by the teenager, Cobb stayed in separate hotels on the road and even carried a gun. Despite the open hostilities from teammates, he batted .316 in 98 games as a 19-year-old in 1906. When he returned to Georgia for the offseason, people noticed a moody, short-tempered man clearly hardened by the experience. He would enjoy a breakout year in 1907, playing with a fury the game had never before seen.

GEORGE DAVIS 1890

Future Hall of Famer George Davis was not the only teenager in the regular lineup for the National League's Cleveland Spiders in 1890. With the 5-foot-9, switch-hitting Davis in center field and fresh-faced Will Smalley at the hot corner, the Spiders — who had finished in sixth place the previous season — had plenty of youth in their favor.

HR	RBI	AVG	H
6	73	.264	139

It was the first and only time in Major League history that a pair of teenage rookies played 100 games apiece, both appearing in all 136 of the Spiders' contests. With a powerful throwing arm, Davis led the league in outfield assists with 35 in 1890, all while batting .264 with six home runs, 22 doubles, nine triples, 53 walks and 73 RBI. He even managed to do a little damage on the basepaths, finishing the season with 22 stolen bases. Yet it wasn't until Aug. 23 of that year that he celebrated his 20th birthday.

Davis's strong arm prompted a transition to third base in 1892 (and later to shortstop). The Spiders were in need of a solid third baseman, as Smalley — who didn't have quite as much success that first season, batting just .213 — had tragically died of a kidney ailment in 1891 at age 20.

Conigliaro

TONY CONIGLIARO 1964

A handsome Bostonian, "Tony C" became an immediate favorite of Red Sox fans when he reached the Majors on April 16, 1964, three months after his 19th birthday. Like most teenagers, Conigliaro slept a lot — as much as 12 hours a night — and hung out with buddies rather than adults.

"You have to learn that the other guys on the team just don't want to go to a dance party and twist or something," he said.

HR	RBI	AVG	SLG
24	52	.290	.530

That spring, Ted Williams projected Conigliaro was two years away from the Bigs. But the teenager played well, and got called up when injuries mounted. Conigliaro responded by hitting .290 with 24 homers and 52 RBI in 111 games. A prospect with limitless potential at age 19, he already had a cult following.

CESAR CEDENO 1970

Unlike the countless other baseball-crazed children that would later grow up in the Dominican Republic dreaming of playing in the Majors, Cesar Cedeno did not spend his 1960s childhood immersed in the game.

His father wanted him to work in the family store, and Cesar didn't begin to learn to play baseball until age 11, when his mother bought him a glove and spikes. At 15, he was sitting on a bench in a Santo Domingo junior league where teams played only on Sundays.

"I probably hadn't played as many as 100 games when I was signed," he would later say. That made his quick ascent to the Major Leagues all the more impressive. As a 17-year-old Houston Astros prospect in 1968, Cedeno batted .374 at Covington (Va.) in the Appalachian League, using many of his off hours learning English by watching *The Flintstones* on television. In 1970, he hit .373 with 14 homers in 54 games for Oklahoma City before Astros management deemed him ready for "the call" up to Houston.

A five-tool talent, the 19-year-old Cedeno batted .310 in 90 games at the Big League level, with 42 RBI, 21 doubles and 17 stolen bases. He played mostly center field as a rookie, showing the range and speed that later would produce five consecutive Gold Glove Awards. Despite beginning the year at Triple-A in 1970, Cedeno finished fourth in NL Rookie of the Year voting behind Expos pitcher Carl Morton, Reds outfielder Bernie Carbo and Phillies shortstop Larry Bowa. Not bad for a teenager still learning the finer points of the game.

HR	RBI	AVG	H
7	42	.310	110

DWIGHT GOODEN 1984

By 1984, baseball fans had grown accustomed to rookie pitchers taking over the game. There was the eclectic Mark "The Bird" Fidrych of the Tigers in 1976, and five years later, Mexican left-hander Fernando Valenzuela generated "Fernandomania" with his whirling, eyes-to-the-sky delivery for the Dodgers.

Playing on the New York stage for a rapidly improving team under rookie Manager Davey Johnson, Dwight "Doc" Gooden might have been even bigger. He gave Mets fans something to cheer about for the first time in a decade.

Although a skinny 19-year-old rookie, Gooden was an imposing figure on the hill with his 6-foot-3 frame and blistering fastball. As with Fidrych and Valenzuela, every Gooden start was an event, and fans arrived at Shea Stadium with stacks of "K" placards to post after each of "Dr. K's" many strikeouts.

W	L	ERA	K
17	9	2.60	276

Opponents compared him to a young Bob Gibson, Tom Seaver or J.R. Richard. Expos first baseman Pete Rose, who had faced Sandy Koufax, said Gooden's fastball rose like that of the legendary Dodgers lefty.

"Only one or two come along in a generation who've got what he's got," said Mets first baseman Keith Hernandez. "He's just 19 and it's so hard to believe."

The youngest of Dan and Ella May Gooden's children by more than a decade, Doc began playing baseball in Tampa, Fla., at the age of 3. He is one of several talented ballplayers to have reached the Majors via Hillsborough High School.

Johnson lobbied Mets brass to put the teenager on the Opening Day roster in '84, a decision made easy after Gooden looked dominant in Spring Training. He finished the season with a 17-9 record and a league-best 276 strikeouts, shattering Herb Score's 29-year-old Big League record for rookies.

Gooden was named NL Rookie of the Year before he even turned 20 on Nov. 16.

Opponents compared him to Bob Gibson, Tom Seaver or J.R. Richard. Pete Rose, who had faced Sandy Koufax, said Gooden's fastball rose like that of the legendary Dodgers lefty.

WALTER JOHNSON 1907

JIMMIE FOXX 1927

The perennially struggling Washington Senators signed 19-year-old Walter Johnson sight unseen out of an Idaho town league in the summer of 1907. *The Washington Post* heralded the arrival of the "phenom" and the "Idaho Wonder."

In his Big League debut on Aug. 2, Johnson faced a Ty Cobb–led Detroit Tigers team that was slugging its way to the first of three straight AL pennants. Johnson allowed just six hits in the hard-luck, 3-2 loss, typical of the rest of his season. He posted

W	L	ERA	K
5	9	1.88	71

a 1.88 ERA over 110.1 innings, but managed just a 5-9 record. Still, the player who would eventually be given the nickname "Big Train" left an impression.

"The first time I faced him, I watched him take that easy wind-up — and then something went past me that made me flinch," Cobb said. "I hardly saw the pitch, but I heard it. The thing just hissed with danger. Every one of us knew we'd met the most powerful arm ever turned loose in a ballpark."

Jimmie Foxx was barely 17-and-a-half years old when he made his debut for the Philadelphia Athletics as a pinch-hitter on May 1, 1925. In February of that year, he had left his classmates at Sudlersville (Md.) High to join the A's for Spring Training in Fort Myers, Fla. Sportswriters noted his ability to handle pitchers, his maturity behind the plate and even his speed.

The Sporting News, which first mentioned the young slugger

HR	RBI	AVG	H
3	20	.323	42

in its Dec. 13, 1924, issue, misspelled his last name in articles until early in 1926. Perhaps the "Bible of Baseball" could be forgiven, since it was not until the 1928 season that Foxx, at the age of 20, began to truly establish himself on the national level.

Yet Foxx's first significant playing time came when he was 19 in 1927. In 146 plate appearances that year, he hit .323 with a .393 OBP. In parts of three seasons in the Majors as a teenager, Foxx batted .339 with three homers and 25 RBI, making sure that at least everyone in Philadelphia knew his name.

YOUNT'S HELMET

ROBIN YOUNT 1974

Raised in Southern California at a time when the cut-off date for school was Jan. 1, Robin Yount was three months shy of his 18th birthday when the Brewers drafted the recent high school graduate with the third overall pick in June 1973.

When Brewers Manager Del Crandall took a look at the shortstop fielding ground balls one day the next March, he turned to club Vice President Jim Wilson and asked, "Is there any reason why an 18-year-old kid can't play shortstop in the Big Leagues?"

Wilson didn't think so, and Yount made his Big League debut on April 5, 1974, more than four months before his 19th birthday.

HR	RBI	AVG	H
3	26	.250	86

He became the team's regular shortstop early in the season, taking over the position from incumbent Tim Johnson. But Yount batted just .250 as a rookie. He also committed 63 errors in his first two years, not yet displaying the skills that would earn him a Gold Glove in 1982.

Still, the MVP potential was there. Hank Aaron, upon joining the Brewers in '75, called Yount the best prospect in baseball. That year, Yount played in 147 games, batting .267 with eight homers and 52 RBI. On Sept. 14, 1975, he played in his 242nd game before turning 20, breaking Mel Ott's 47-year-old record for games played in the Bigs as a teenager.

TEENAGERS

BOB FELLER 1936

Raised on an Iowa farm playing catch between the family farmhouse and barn, Bob Feller could throw a curve at age 8. At 13, he and his father, Bill, cut down about 20 oak trees to carve out their own field of dreams. At 17, Feller signed with the Indians; the Cleveland scout, Cy Slapnicka, was a down-to-earth Iowan with whom his family could relate.

In this pre-radar gun era, Feller threw an estimated 100 mph, earning the nicknames "The Heater from Van Meter" and "Rapid Robert." With his trademark windmill wind-up and repertoire of fastball, slider and curve, he struck out 15 St. Louis Browns in his first Big League start on Aug. 23, 1936, one shy of the AL record. On Sept. 13, facing the A's, he struck out a record 17, one batter for each year of his life.

Teenage prodigies were unusual during Feller's era, and "Bobby" was a national curiosity. The press called him "Master Feller" and General Mills hired him to endorse its cereals along with child actress Shirley Temple, the only minor more famous than he. After his rookie season, he returned home to Van Meter High for his senior year.

The following spring, he appeared on the cover of *Time* magazine. NBC radio covered his high school graduation live. In 1937, at age 18, he went 9-7 with a 3.39 ERA and 150 strikeouts in 148.2 innings.

Before Feller struck out 18 Tigers in '38 to set the modern Big League strikeout record. As a 19-year-old that season, he struck out a league-leading 240 batters for the first of seven strikeout titles. By his 20th birthday, he already had amassed 31 wins and 466 K's.

W	L	ERA	IP
5	3	3.34	62

chapter 4

BETTER LATE THAN NEVER

Not every rookie is a 20-year-old prodigy. Some aren't ready for prime time right away or aren't given the opportunity. A generation of baseball's greatest stars spent their best seasons in the Negro Leagues waiting for the game to integrate. Pitchers, forever vulnerable to arm injuries, often must endure rehabilitations or reinvent themselves as submariners or relievers before making their debut. Other players are late bloomers, toiling in the Minors or biding their time until a position opens. Then there are once promising prospects like Jim Morris, who drift away only to return for unlikely second acts.

JIM MORRIS 1999

Jim Morris had long since given up his baseball dream. A first-round pick of the Milwaukee Brewers in 1983, Morris toiled in the Minors until '89, when arm problems seemed to put an end to his career. By the late '90s, the father of three had settled in to a career teaching chemistry and coaching baseball at Reagan County High School in Brownwood, Texas, a tiny town about 100 miles west of Waco.

Before the 1999 season, he told his ballplayers that if they reached the state playoffs, he would attend an open tryout held by the then–Devil Rays. The team went on to reach the playoffs for the first time in school history, and Morris, who had been throwing batting practice without pain, traveled to the tryout without any illusions of impressing scouts at age 35.

At the tryout, Rays scouts were intrigued by his story and asked if he had brought any of his players. The last one to throw, Morris

W	L	ERA	IP
0	0	5.79	4.2

hit 94 on the radar gun, then 95 and finally 98. Tampa Bay, desperate for pitching, signed the lefty on June 23 and assigned him to Double-A. Three months later, he jogged out of the bullpen at Rangers Ballpark in Arlington and struck out Royce Clayton.

Tampa Bay catcher John Flaherty initially thought the story was a hoax, "like that Sidd Finch guy in *Sports Illustrated*."

"We didn't bring him up here because he's a good story," then–Devil Rays Manager Larry Rothschild said of Morris. "We brought him in because he's a left-hander with a good arm."

Morris pitched just 15 innings over 21 relief appearances for the Devil Rays in '99 and 2000 and failed to latch on with the Dodgers in 2001, but he made enough of an impact to launch a third career as a motivational speaker and inspire the Disney movie *The Rookie*, which starred Dennis Quaid as Morris.

DAZZY VANCE 1922

Charles Arthur "Dazzy" Vance won the first of a record seven consecutive NL strikeout titles in 1922, his rookie season. An Iowa native who didn't become a fixture in the Majors until age 31, Vance developed his skills playing a rudimentary version of the sport with his brother on the family farm.

"We didn't have a great deal of time to play, for there was plowing, hoeing, milking and other chores to be done," Vance said.

Vance earned cups of coffee with the Pirates and Yankees in 1915 and again with the Yankees three years later, but each time he would tire by midseason and be sent back down. After an arm operation, his manager in New Orleans had him start on four days' rest instead of the usual three. The extra day turned his career around. Vance posted a 21-11 mark in the Southern Association in 1921 and was purchased by the Dodgers, who didn't realize their good fortune. Owner Charlie Ebbets wanted Hank DeBerry, Vance's catcher, but was persuaded to take the pitcher as a package deal.

Ebbets was later grateful for the throw-in. One of the few Major League pitchers of his era to attack batters with a straight overhand delivery, Vance went 18-12 for the Dodgers in 1922, leading the NL in strikeouts (134) and shutouts (5).

Vance placed fifth in the NL in hits per nine innings with 9.489, an impressive figure considering the league hit .292 that season. In consecutive starts in late May, Vance shut out the Cubs and then the Phillies, even with the second game being played in the hitter-friendly confines of the Baker Bowl in Philadelphia.

W	L	ERA	IP
18	12	3.70	245.2

HOYT WILHELM 1952

As a 12-year-old in rural North Carolina, Hoyt Wilhelm taught himself the knuckleball after reading about four Washington Senators who threw the pitch. Practicing with a tennis ball initially, Wilhelm would eventually become one of the masters of the pitch.

Even with the knuckler in his repertoire, Wilhelm did not join the New York Giants until three months shy of his 30th birthday. Between his seven years in the Minors and service time in World War II — he was awarded a Purple Heart at the Battle of the Bulge in 1944 — Wilhelm didn't make his Big League debut until 1952.

On April 23, 1952, in his second Big League game and first at-bat, Wilhelm homered against the Boston Braves at the Polo Grounds for what would be the only

W	L	ERA	IP
15	3	2.43	159.1

round-tripper of his career. He also pitched five innings in relief to get his first win.

Wilhelm threw 159.1 innings that year, a rookie record for relievers. He led the NL in games (71) and ERA (2.43), and his 15-3 record produced a league-high .833 winning percentage. He narrowly lost the Rookie of the Year Award to fellow reliever Joe Black of the Dodgers, who also won 15 games. Wilhelm also finished fourth in the NL Most Valuable Player voting behind Black, Cubs outfielder Hank Sauer and Phillies pitcher Robin Roberts.

ELSTON HOWARD 1955

Like many African-American players of his era, Elston Howard spent part of his professional career in the Negro Leagues while waiting for the Majors to integrate. After passing up collegiate baseball, Howard made his professional debut with the Kansas City Monarchs in 1948.

Howard spent three seasons as an outfielder playing for Manager Buck O'Neil's Monarchs and rooming with future Cubs Hall of Famer Ernie Banks. In 1950, the St. Louis native inked his first Minor League deal, becoming one of the first African-American players to be purchased by the New York Yankees.

Howard spent four seasons in the Minors, winning the International League Most Valuable Player Award while with Toronto in 1954. Even though the Yankees had perennial MVP candidate Yogi Berra behind the plate, coach Bill Dickey worked with Howard at becoming a catcher.

HR	RBI	AVG	SLG
10	43	.290	.477

In 1955, Howard finally reached the Major Leagues, becoming the first black player to wear Yankees pinstripes. The 26-year-old made his Big League debut on April 14, singling in his first at-bat in an 8-4 loss to the Red Sox at Fenway Park.

With Berra in the midst of his third MVP season, Howard caught just nine games as a rookie, seeing most of his time in the outfield. He batted .290 with 10 home runs and 43 RBI in 97 games. In his first World Series at-bat, he hit a three-run homer against the Dodgers.

A humble, soft-spoken man, Howard never objected to biding his time behind Berra and waiting for a regular role in the Yankees' potent lineup. In fact, he and Berra, a fellow St. Louis native, became close friends.

"Class was the way to describe the guy," said teammate Dick Howser.

MLB MVPs WHO ALSO PLAYED IN THE NEGRO LEAGUES	
PLAYER	MVP YEAR(S)
Jackie Robinson	1949
Roy Campanella	1951, 1953, 1955
Willie Mays	1954
Don Newcombe	1956
Hank Aaron	1957
Ernie Banks	1958, 1959
Elston Howard	**1963**

BETTER LATE THAN NEVER

JOE McGINNITY 1899

"Iron Man" Joe McGinnity, known for his longevity and endurance, actually was a late bloomer. Born in 1871, he spent two unsuccessful seasons in the Minors before quitting professional baseball in 1894 to run a saloon. As a hard-nosed saloon manager, McGinnity never had to hire a bouncer, and he brought that same demeanor to the mound. During the next three years, he pitched sandlot ball and developed a variety of curveballs with a submarine delivery he claimed was easy on the arm.

"McGinnity was a magician in the box," said Hall-of-Fame Manager Connie Mack. "It was difficult for a batter to get his measure. Sometimes his fingers would almost scrape the ground as he hurled the ball. He knew all the tricks for putting a batter on the spot."

He belatedly broke into the Majors with the Baltimore Orioles in 1899 at age 28. Pitching for Manager John McGraw, McGinnity led the National League in victories, posting a 28-16 record in 48 games, including 41 starts. His 2.68 ERA ranked third in the league, and his 366.1 innings ranked fourth, although he would lead the league in innings pitched four times during the next five seasons.

Although McGinnity's nickname might have come from his work at an iron foundry, his durability certainly solidified him as the "Iron Man." He started both games of a doubleheader three times in a single month in 1903.

When the NL cut back from 12 teams to eight in 1900, the Orioles were dropped and McGinnity was awarded to Brooklyn. There, the Iron Man would continue to make up for lost time.

W	L	ERA	IP
28	16	2.68	366.1

Easter

LUKE EASTER 1950

The gregarious, 6-foot-4 Luscious Luke Easter was a Negro Leagues veteran when Cleveland Indians Owner Bill Veeck purchased his contract from the Homestead Grays in 1949. Despite a midseason knee operation, Easter batted .363 with 25 homers in the Pacific Coast League, prompting the Tribe to trade All-Star Mickey Vernon to open first base.

HR	RBI	AVG	SLG
28	107	.280	.487

Easter hit .280 as a 34-year-old rookie in 1950 with 28 home runs and 107 RBI. He and Al Rosen are one of just three sets of rookie teammates ever to drive in 100 runs each. Many believe Easter's power rivaled that of Josh Gibson and Babe Ruth. When a fan mentioned that he once witnessed Easter's longest home run, Easter replied, "If it came down, it wasn't my longest."

WILCY MOORE 1927

Perhaps the best pitcher on the greatest team of all time was a little known 30-year-old, side-arming rookie who emerged from the bullpen to embarrass hitters with his deadly sinker. Pitching for the heralded 1927 New York Yankees, Wilcy Moore was one of the game's first "firemen," a reliever who came in with the game on the line and runners on base. On a team renowned for its prodigious power, Moore was the secret weapon deployed when an opponent managed to keep things close.

Moore arrived late to the Majors after breaking his arm two years earlier, forcing him to adopt a side-armed delivery. The Texan finished his rookie season 19-7 with 13 saves. Despite posting a league-leading 2.28 ERA, Moore was not considered to have won the AL's ERA title that year because the rules of the day required pitchers to have 10 complete games and Moore tossed just six. Still, he and Joe Black (1952) are the only rookies to win at least 13 games and save at least 13 others.

In the 1927 World Series against Pittsburgh, Moore notched a save in Game 1 and threw a complete game in the decisive Game 4, but he never replicated his rookie success and pitched just parts of five more seasons.

On a team renowned for its prodigious power, Moore was the secret weapon deployed when an opponent managed to keep things close.

W	L	ERA	SV
19	7	2.28	13

chapter 5

LAND OF THE RISING STARS

For decades, baseball fans and insiders debated the merits of Japanese players relative to their Big League counterparts. The only player to make the leap from Japan to the Majors before the 1990s, Masonori Murakami, had pitched briefly for the San Francisco Giants in 1964 and '65. Japanese players were bound to their home league by rules that made it difficult to depart, but in 1995, Hideo Nomo found a loophole that enabled him to sign with the Dodgers. His success opened the door, and soon every team was pursuing top Japanese talent.

HIDEO NOMO 1995

Hideo Nomo had a nation's hopes riding on his right arm in 1995. He did not disappoint. Exploiting a technicality in the rules intended to keep Japanese players in domestic leagues, he retired from the Kintetsu Buffaloes and signed with the Los Angeles Dodgers.

Nicknamed "The Tornado" in Japan for his whirling, herky-jerky delivery, the 26-year-old brought a much-needed diversion to a sport coming off its longest work stoppage. More than 100 Japanese media traveled with the Dodgers, who hired a full-time interpreter to accommodate them. Nomo's starts were front-page news in Japan. Japan's NHK public TV network broadcast his games live. Nomo won seven of his first eight decisions in 1995, started the All-Star Game, and triggered a wave of "Nomomania" that rivaled "Fernandomania" in 1981.

W	L	ERA	K
13	6	2.54	236

"It's bigger than Fernando Valenzuela," said Manager Tommy Lasorda. "Fernando didn't have much media following him. Hideo has a whole country."

Not since Luis Tiant had baseball seen a delivery as unorthodox as Nomo's. First, he threw his arms up, as if grabbing a bar, while thrusting his chest forward. After holding the pose briefly, he twisted toward second, turning his back to the batter. Finally, he whirled around, delivering a forkball, curve or fastball. "It takes a few pitches to figure him out," said the Mets' Brett Butler. "And he's wild enough to keep you on your toes."

Nomo led the NL in strikeouts (236) while going 13-6. Although some baseball writers believed a veteran of the Japanese Leagues should not be accorded rookie status, Nomo easily defeated Atlanta's Chipper Jones for Rookie of the Year honors, becoming the fourth consecutive Dodger to win the award.

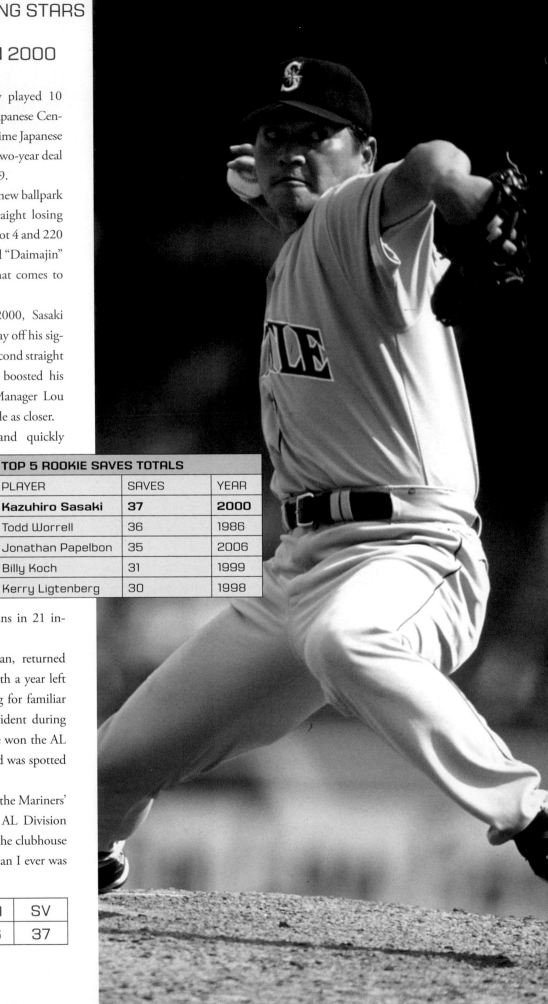

LAND OF THE RISING STARS

KAZUHIRO SASAKI 2000

Kazuhiro Sasaki had already played 10 seasons for Yokohama in the Japanese Central League and owned the all-time Japanese saves record when he signed a two-year deal with Seattle in December 1999.

The Mariners, playing in a new ballpark and coming off a second straight losing season, needed a boost. At 6 foot 4 and 220 pounds, Sasaki was nicknamed "Daimajin" after a giant stone samurai that comes to life in a Japanese movie.

After a strong start in 2000, Sasaki slumped as hitters learned to lay off his signature forkball. Following a second straight ninth-inning meltdown that boosted his ERA to 7.36 in late May, Manager Lou Piniella stripped him of his role as closer.

Sasaki was undaunted and quickly earned back his job by spotting the forkball for strikes and becoming more aggressive with a fastball that gained speed as the season wore on. He saved a rookie-record 37 games, blowing just three chances, and allowed two runs in 21 innings leading into the ALCS.

Sasaki, homesick for Japan, returned east after the 2003 season with a year left on his contract. That longing for familiar surroundings was not yet evident during the 2000 campaign, when he won the AL Rookie of the Year Award and was spotted frequently around Seattle.

After saving two games in the Mariners' sweep of the White Sox in AL Division Series play, Sasaki reveled in the clubhouse celebration. "I am happier than I ever was in Japan," he said.

TOP 5 ROOKIE SAVES TOTALS		
PLAYER	SAVES	YEAR
Kazuhiro Sasaki	**37**	**2000**
Todd Worrell	36	1986
Jonathan Papelbon	35	2006
Billy Koch	31	1999
Kerry Ligtenberg	30	1998

W	L	ERA	SV
2	5	3.16	37

HIDEKI MATSUI 2003

Hideki Matsui was the first Japanese player to arrive in the Big Leagues with a reputation as a power hitter, having blasted 50 homers in Japan in 2002. Belting a grand slam in the Yankees' home opener on April 8, the player dubbed "Godzilla" made an immediate impact.

With Japanese media tracking his every step, Matsui did not match his typical output, but he did bat .287 with 16 homers and 106 RBI. He appeared in the All-Star Game and also validated his reputation for durability. After playing in 1,250 straight contests for the Yomiuri Giants, he appeared in a rookie-record 163 in '03.

HR	RBI	AVG	H
16	106	.287	179

Like many Japanese rookies, Matsui experienced culture shock. He lived alone in a Manhattan high-rise, ate mostly at Japanese restaurants, and socialized mostly with Japanese writers and friends. Still, he deftly dealt with the media and was popular among teammates and fans. *People* magazine even named him one of its "Men We Love."

Although three Japanese players had previously won Rookie of the Year honors, the debate over whether a Japan League veteran should be eligible for the award reached a crescendo in 2003. Two voters admitted to leaving Matsui off their ballot altogether, and the award went to the Royals' Angel Berroa.

ICHIRO'S BAT

ICHIRO SUZUKI 2001

Prior to the 2001 season, Ichiro Suzuki became the first Japanese position player to sign with a Major League club. At the time he joined the Mariners, ballplayers from the Far East tended to have a more slight build than their Western counterparts and generally were regarded as too small to compete anywhere but on the pitcher's mound.

Few knew what to expect from the 5-foot-9, 160-pound outfielder, who had won the previous seven batting titles in the Japanese Pacific League playing for the Orix Blue Wave. Scouts recommended busting the left-handed hitter with inside fastballs.

Instead, he baffled pitchers with his slashing, lunging batting stroke. He punched balls through gaps as if wielding a pool cue or tennis racket instead of a black Mizuno bat. So fast was Ichiro — he asked to be called only by his first name — that any lazy ground ball became a potential hit.

"He can hit *anything*," Yankees pitcher Andy Pettitte once lamented. "You just

H	RBI	AVG	SB
242	69	.350	56

have to hope he hits it up in the air, because he's so fast he beats out groundballs."

Ichiro hit .336 in April and .370 in May, proving that his Japanese numbers were legitimate. Then there was his powerful, accurate cannon of a right-field arm, which earned him comparisons to Roberto Clemente and other all-time great defensive players. He was voted to start in the All-Star Game and responded with a single off ex-Mariner Randy Johnson at Safeco Field.

In the season after superstar shortstop Alex Rodriguez left Seattle as a free agent, Ichiro drove the '01 Mariners to an AL-record 116 wins by leading the American League in batting (.350), steals (56) and hits — setting a rookie record with 242 — while winning both the AL Most Valuable Player and Rookie of the Year awards. In doing so, he not only proved that Japanese position players could compete in the Majors, but also that they could rank among the best.

DAISUKE MATSUZAKA 2007

No Japanese player arrived in the Majors with more hoopla than Daisuke Matsuzaka. The Red Sox paid $51.1 million for the right to negotiate with him, and $52 million (over six years) to actually sign him.

The product of a Japanese pitching culture much different than that of U.S. baseball, Matsuzaka threw 200-pitch bullpen sessions and routinely reached 140 pitches in games. In Japan, he went 108-60 with a 2.95 ERA while averaging a complete game every 2.8 starts.

Japan's Seibu Lions signed Matsuzaka out of high school in 1998 even though the Colorado Rockies and Arizona Diamondbacks pursued him. In November 2006, Boston outbid everyone for a righty who was believed to have at least eight pitches in his arsenal.

W	L	ERA	IP
15	12	4.40	204.2

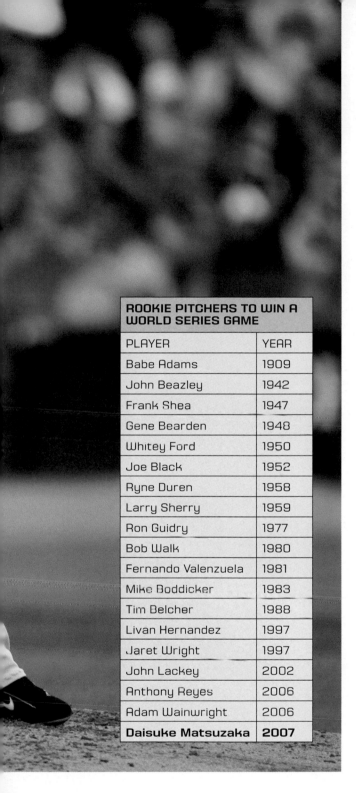

ROOKIE PITCHERS TO WIN A WORLD SERIES GAME	
PLAYER	YEAR
Babe Adams	1909
John Beazley	1942
Frank Shea	1947
Gene Bearden	1948
Whitey Ford	1950
Joe Black	1952
Ryne Duren	1958
Larry Sherry	1959
Ron Guidry	1977
Bob Walk	1980
Fernando Valenzuela	1981
Mike Boddicker	1983
Tim Belcher	1988
Livan Hernandez	1997
Jaret Wright	1997
John Lackey	2002
Anthony Reyes	2006
Adam Wainwright	2006
Daisuke Matsuzaka	**2007**

Matsuzaka used a wind-up unlike any taught in America. He swung his hands over his head, paused, and lowered his hands as he turned on the mound. From there, he paused again, and then unleashed the ball in a violent delivery in which he dropped so low that his right knee sometimes scraped the mound.

As a rookie, Matsuzaka won 15 games, had 201 strikeouts and won Game 3 of Boston's World Series sweep of Colorado.

TAKASHI SAITO 2006

Unlike many of his countrymen, Japanese star Takashi Saito arrived in the Majors with little fanfare. The 6-foot-1 right-hander left Japan after the 2005 season, signed a $500,000 Minor League contract with the Los Angeles Dodgers, and did not even make the Big League club out of Spring Training. Yet he inherited the closer role that May and set a franchise rookie record with 24 saves.

One of the oldest Dodgers rookies ever at age 36, Saito was a four-time All-Star in Japan, but since he was a free agent, the Dodgers did not have to post a fee to earn the rights to sign him. Given what Boston paid ($51.1 million) just to *negotiate* with

W	L	ERA	SV
6	2	2.07	24

Daisuke Matsuzaka the next year, Saito proved to be a bargain.

Saito had never been a full-time closer during his 14-year career with Japan's Yokohama BayStars. He brought a low-90s fastball to the Bigs, along with a splitter, but his best weapon was a deceptive slider that he often got batters to chase out of the strike zone.

Saito went 6-2 with a 2.07 ERA and converted all but two save chances. He struck out 107 batters in 78.1 innings and limited opponents to a .177 average; right-handed batters hit just .129 off of him. The former non-roster player finished seventh in Rookie of the Year balloting and eighth in voting for the Cy Young Award.

chapter 6
CHARISMA

Some rookies don't dazzle just with their talents. They bring boyish enthusiasm, quirky habits and unorthodox deliveries. The result is an infectious mix that can become a national phenomenon. Often the magnetic personality presents itself in the form of a pitcher, further fueling the excitement by appearing only every fourth or fifth day. From Satchel Paige to Mark Fidrych, Minnie Minoso to Ken Griffey Jr., baseball has produced an abundance of charismatic rookies. These ballplayers brought a joie de vivre that energized teammates, coaches and fans alike.

MARK FIDRYCH 1976

Arguably the most colorful first-year player in baseball history, Mark Fidrych took baseball by storm in the summer of 1976. A gangly 6-foot-3 righty with unkempt curls, he was nicknamed "The Bird" because he resembled *Sesame Street*'s "Big Bird," with whom he appeared on the cover of *Sports Illustrated*.

During games, Fidrych would talk to the baseball, bend down and groom the mound with his hands and slap high-fives with teammates in the middle of the diamond after good defensive plays. Such behavior might not have been noticed if the gregarious 21-year-old were not such a precocious talent.

W	L	ERA	IP
19	9	2.34	250.1

He arrived in the Majors less than two years after the Tigers chose him in the 10th round of the 1974 draft, making the '76 Opening Day roster after entering Spring Training as a non-roster invitee. Fidrych's starts became must-see events, not only at Tiger Stadium but also on the road.

Detroit finished fifth in the AL East in 1976, but the Tigers' attendance rose 400,000 from '75, largely due to Fidrych. The team averaged 18,000 more fans for his starts than for other games, and his outings accounted for more than 40 percent of total attendance.

In a nationally televised game against the Yankees at Tiger Stadium on June 28, Fidrych tossed a complete-game seven-hitter. Strutting around the mound and talking to the ball, he became a national sensation. Two weeks later, he started the All-Star Game for the AL. He finished 19-9 as a rookie, led the league in ERA (2.34) and complete games (24), and was runner-up to the Orioles' Jim Palmer in the Cy Young voting. Unfortunately, arm injuries derailed a promising career. He would start just 27 more games before hanging up his spikes after the 1980 season.

"He was the game's Pied Piper, the most charismatic player I've seen," Tigers Hall-of-Fame announcer Ernie Harwell said in 2001.

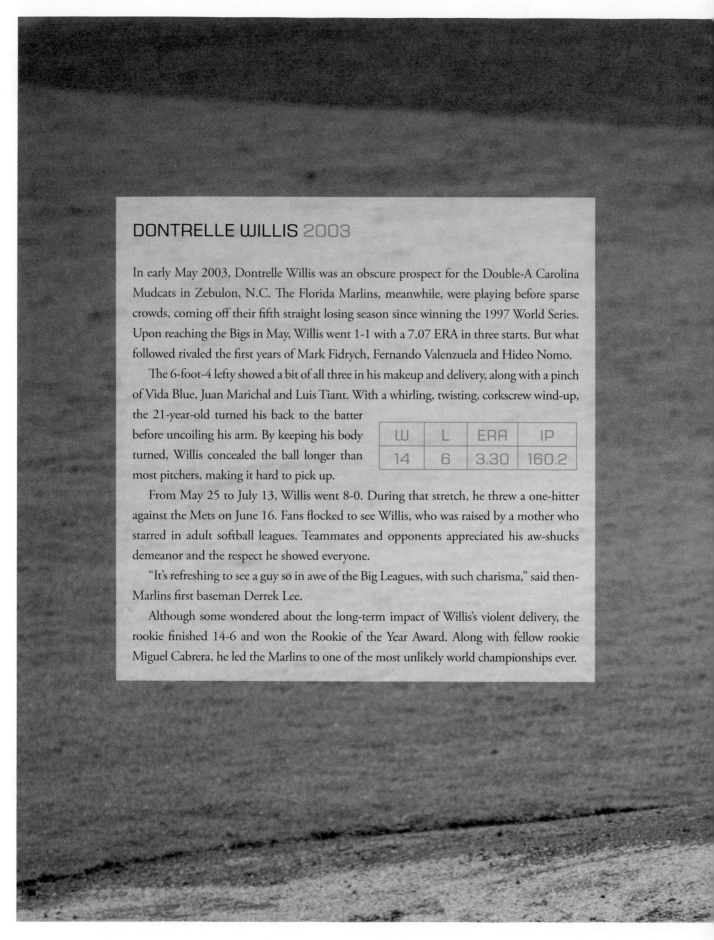

DONTRELLE WILLIS 2003

In early May 2003, Dontrelle Willis was an obscure prospect for the Double-A Carolina Mudcats in Zebulon, N.C. The Florida Marlins, meanwhile, were playing before sparse crowds, coming off their fifth straight losing season since winning the 1997 World Series. Upon reaching the Bigs in May, Willis went 1-1 with a 7.07 ERA in three starts. But what followed rivaled the first years of Mark Fidrych, Fernando Valenzuela and Hideo Nomo.

The 6-foot-4 lefty showed a bit of all three in his makeup and delivery, along with a pinch of Vida Blue, Juan Marichal and Luis Tiant. With a whirling, twisting, corkscrew wind-up, the 21-year-old turned his back to the batter before uncoiling his arm. By keeping his body turned, Willis concealed the ball longer than most pitchers, making it hard to pick up.

W	L	ERA	IP
14	6	3.30	160.2

From May 25 to July 13, Willis went 8-0. During that stretch, he threw a one-hitter against the Mets on June 16. Fans flocked to see Willis, who was raised by a mother who starred in adult softball leagues. Teammates and opponents appreciated his aw-shucks demeanor and the respect he showed everyone.

"It's refreshing to see a guy so in awe of the Big Leagues, with such charisma," said then-Marlins first baseman Derrek Lee.

Although some wondered about the long-term impact of Willis's violent delivery, the rookie finished 14-6 and won the Rookie of the Year Award. Along with fellow rookie Miguel Cabrera, he led the Marlins to one of the most unlikely world championships ever.

Griffey Sr. (left),
Griffey Jr.

KEN GRIFFEY JR. 1989

Ken Griffey Jr. was supposed to spend 1989 in the Minors. That was what the Mariners had planned for the top pick in the 1987 draft — another year of seasoning for the son of the "Big Red Machine" outfielder.

The demotion was such a foregone conclusion that only one of the five major baseball trading card manufacturers included Griffey in its 1989 card set. But when the 19-year-old batted .359 and set team records with 33 hits and 21 RBI in Spring Training, both the Mariners and Upper Deck officials realized they had a Big League product on their hands.

"Junior" grew up in Big League clubhouses and treated his rookie season like just another day at the park. With his youthful energy, ever-present smile and tendency to wear his hat backward during batting practice, it was no wonder teammates called him "The Kid."

At 6 foot 3 and 195 pounds, with a beautiful left-handed upper-cut swing, he showed great potential as a power hitter. But his defense drew bigger raves. Gliding toward balls in center field, he once crashed into Fenway Park's Green Monster to rob Wade Boggs of a hit. Another time, he threw out Robin Yount trying to stretch a triple, firing a strike to third from 375 feet away.

In 1989, Junior and Griffey Sr. made history as the first father-son tandem to play in the Majors at the same time. Junior batted .264 with 16 homers and 61 RBI, finishing third in AL Rookie of the Year voting.

"He's a big kid, a baby," said Gene Clines, the Mariners' hitting coach. "When he finally buckles down and gets serious about this game, there's no telling what kind of numbers he will put on the board."

HR	RBI	AVG	SLG
16	61	.264	.420

FERNANDO VALENZUELA
1981

When Jerry Reuss was unavailable at the last minute for the Dodgers' season opener against the Astros in 1981, Manager Tommy Lasorda turned to a 20-year-old Mexican left-hander with a quirky delivery.

And thus began "Fernandomania."

Throwing the most effective screwball in the league, Fernando Valenzuela blanked the Astros in his first start. He tossed a one-run complete game in his next outing before rattling off three shutouts. All told, he won his first eight starts, allowing just four runs.

The Dodgers tapped into the local Latino market, with fans packing Dodger Stadium whenever Valenzuela pitched. On the road, the team held news conferences before each series to deal with the media crush.

Slightly pudgy at 5 foot 11 and 190 pounds, Valenzuela utilized his weight on the mound. Catcher Mike Scioscia marveled that he seemed to get stronger as the game progressed.

Using a high leg kick, Valenzuela's eyes went skyward as he delivered. Although he threw a plus curve and a hard fastball, it was the screwball (which he threw 60 percent of the time) that gave batters fits.

"I'm in awe of anybody who can master the screwball," said the Astros' Don Sutton.

Only the 50-day players strike could slow Valenzuela down. When the season resumed, he started the All-Star Game for the NL and finished 13-7 on the year, leading the NL in starts, innings, K's, shutouts and complete games. He won the Rookie of the Year Award and became the first rookie to capture the Cy Young Award. He also won three playoff games, helping the Dodgers to their first world title since 1965.

W	L	ERA	IP
13	7	2.48	192.1

MINNIE MINOSO 1951

When Cuban-born Minnie Minoso took the field for the White Sox on May 1, 1951, he made history as the first black player in the Majors for a Chicago team. Facing the Yankees' hard-throwing Vic Raschi with a runner on first and no outs, Minoso took the first pitch, then sent the second one into the center-field bullpen.

Already 25, Minoso had taken a roundabout path to the Majors. A Negro Leagues standout, he was acquired by Bill Veeck's Cleveland Indians prior to the 1948 season and made his Big League debut the next season, appearing in nine games.

Minoso was sent back to the Minors, where he stayed until the beginning of the 1951 season. Traded to the White Sox in part of a three-team, seven-player deal involving the Philadelphia Athletics, he initially felt hurt and betrayed.

HR	RBI	AVG	OBP
10	76	.326	.422

Those feelings dissipated as he blossomed in Chicago, dazzling fans with his all-around play. As a rookie, he batted .326 with 10 home runs and 76 RBI and appeared in the All-Star Game. Minoso led the AL in triples (14), steals (31) and hit by pitches (16), three categories in which he would be a perennial leader throughout his career.

Minoso finished second in the AL batting race to the A's Ferris Fain, lost a close Rookie of the Year vote to Yankee Gil McDougald, and was fourth in MVP voting.

SATCHEL PAIGE 1948

Some people thought it was unfair that Jackie Robinson — and not Satchel Paige — broke baseball's color barrier. After all, it was the legendary, eccentric Paige — widely considered the best pitcher of any race during his prime — who was the biggest drawing card in the Negro Leagues.

But Paige already was past 40 years of age when Robinson, 28 years old at the time, debuted for the Brooklyn Dodgers in 1947. The following season, Bill Veeck's Cleveland Indians needed pitching help late in the year. Veeck gave Paige a tryout on the right-hander's 42nd birthday, placing a cigarette on the ground to be used as an imaginary home plate.

Paige fired five fastballs, four of which sailed directly over the cigarette. Two days later, he became the Big Leagues' oldest rookie. Still a draw, Paige attracted a crowd of 78,382 to Cleveland on Aug. 20 to see him pitch his second consecutive three-hit shutout.

W	L	ERA	IP
6	1	2.48	72.2

Paige finished the '48 campaign with a 6-1 record in 21 appearances as a middle-aged rookie, providing a late-season boost to the eventual World Series–champion Indians. There was talk of Paige receiving the Rookie of the Year honor, an idea he dismissed, hinting that he would not accept it. Because of his advanced age, perhaps voters shared his sentiment. Both the Major League Baseball and *The Sporting News* versions of the award went to other players.

As Paige recalled in his autobiography, a sportswriter told him after the Aug. 20 game that he looked to be in good shape for his age.

"You should have seen me five or six years ago," Paige said. "I was twice as good as I am now."

OLDEST ROOKIES TO MAKE MLB DEBUT			
PLAYER	AGE	YEAR	TEAM
Satchel Paige	**42**	**1948**	**Cleveland Indians**
Diomedes Olivo	41	1960	Pittsburgh Pirates
John Greening	40	1888	Washington Nationals
Ed Green	40	1890	Philadelphia Athletics
Chuck Hostetler	40	1944	Detroit Tigers
Ken Takahashi	40	2009	New York Mets

chapter 7

BLASTING ONTO THE SCENE

As rookie phenoms go, there's nothing more exciting than a fuzzy-cheeked slugger launching home runs off veteran pitchers. Such first-year sluggers are among the rarest of breeds. Buck Freeman had pitched briefly in 1891 for Washington and then re-emerged as one of the game's top power hitters after seven years in the Minors. Ralph Kiner had barely touched a bat in years when he joined the Pirates fresh off service in World War II. Yankees prospect Kevin Maas began homering at a Ruthian pace after getting called up in 1990, only to tail off quickly. Then there was Mark McGwire, whose 49 home runs as a rookie in 1987 were just the beginning.

KEVIN MAAS 1990

The New York Yankees were in the midst of a four-year stretch of losing seasons when Kevin Maas joined the team midway through 1990, giving Yankees fans hope for a quick turnaround. A 6-foot-3 slugger with a beautiful left-handed swing that seemed tailor-made for Yankee Stadium's short right-field porch, Maas's debut was so awesome that he was soon considered the heir apparent to All-Star Don Mattingly at first base.

A 22nd-round pick in 1986, Maas hit 10 home runs in his first 72 at-bats, reaching that mark, as well as 13 and 15 homers, in fewer at-bats than any other player in Big League history.

HR	RBI	AVG	SLG
21	41	.252	.535

Maas's good looks earned him a large contingent of female fans; some admiring ladies in the right-field stands even donned "Maas tops." Whenever he slugged a homer, the women would remove the tops and cheer. After hitting 18 home runs in 204 at-bats, he was drawing comparisons to the Yankees' all-time greats.

"I'm not trying to fill anybody else's shoes," he said at the time. "I'm not going to try to be the next Babe Ruth."

He wasn't. Although Maas belted 21 home runs in just 254 at-bats that season, finishing second in the Rookie of the Year voting to Cleveland catcher Sandy Alomar Jr., his career quickly tailed off. Maas hit 23 home runs in 1991 but only 21 more throughout the rest of his Big League career, retiring in 1997 after a stint with the Twins and in Japan.

In 1990, Maas was part of a heavy-hitting Yankees roster that included Steve Balboni, Jesse Barfield and fellow rookie Hensley "Bam-Bam" Meulens. The club still won just 67 games, finishing last in the AL East.

"I was hot at the right time," Maas said. "I maybe set myself up for some tough expectations that first year. I wouldn't do it any other way, though. It all worked out for a reason. It was a spectacular way to break in."

BLASTING ONTO THE SCENE

HAL TROSKY 1934

At 6 foot 2 and 207 pounds, Hal Trosky was an imposing figure for the Cleveland Indians as a 21-year-old rookie in 1934.

On May 30, the lefty first baseman from Iowa showed he knew how to make use of his brawn, homering three times in the second game of a doubleheader against the White Sox. On June 14, he smacked another two home runs, including a grand slam, in the Tribe's 11-7 win over the A's.

Playing every inning of all 154 games during the '34 season, Trosky belted 35 homers — then the fifth-highest output by a rookie. He set a rookie record with 142 RBI that Ted Williams would break with 145 in 1939. Trosky finished seventh in MVP balloting that year, not far behind Triple Crown winner Lou Gehrig, who was fifth. His performance helped the Indians improve 10 games from 1933, moving from fourth to third in the AL.

Trosky led first-year players in seemingly every offensive category, including batting (.330), slugging (.598), hits (206), doubles (45), home runs and RBI. His 35 homers were third in the AL behind Gehrig and Jimmie Foxx, and his 142 RBI trailed only Gehrig.

Trosky racked up a rookie-record 89 extra-base hits. His 374 total bases was the rookie standard until 1964, when Tony Oliva matched him. With 206 hits and 142 RBI, Trosky is one of just five rookies to amass 200-plus hits and 100-plus RBI, a group that includes Jimmy Williams (1899), Dale Alexander (1929), Joe DiMaggio (1936) and Frank McCormick (1938).

TOP 5 ROOKIE RBI TOTALS		
PLAYER	RBI	YEAR
Ted Williams	145	1939
Walt Dropo	144	1950
Hal Trosky	**142**	**1934**
Dale Alexander	137	1929
Albert Pujols	130	2001

HR	RBI	AVG	SLG
35	142	.330	.598

BUCK FREEMAN 1899

Professional baseball enjoyed a huge influx of rookie talent in 1899, highlighted by John Frank "Buck" Freeman.

Freeman played briefly for the Washington Statesmen of the American Association as a 19-year-old lefty starter in 1891, going 3-2 with a 3.89 ERA in five games. He spent the next seven seasons toiling in minor leagues before returning to elite competition as a power-hitting right fielder.

In 1899, while with the Washington Senators, he smashed 25 homers, more than twice any other player. Freeman hit his 20th home run, breaking the rookie record, against future Hall of Famer Rube Waddell, and nearly equalled the overall mark of 27 by Ned Willamson in 1884.

Freeman was part of a promising all-rookie outfield for the Senators that included Jimmy Slagle and Jack O'Brien. He hit .318 with 122 RBI, second only to Ed Delahanty.

ALVIN DAVIS 1984

It took the expansion Seattle Mariners eight seasons to develop a homegrown star. Alvin Davis came of age just as a nearby company called Microsoft, founded in 1975, began to make an impact. After taking over at first just seven games into the season, Davis was leading the AL in slugging in early June.

"I've never seen anybody pitched to like they pitched to you in Oakland," Mariners Manager Del Crandall told Davis. "And I played with Hank Aaron and Willie Mays."

HR	RBI	AVG	SLG
27	116	.284	.497

The gregarious rookie was hailed for his maturity and poise at the plate, where he batted .284. Davis won the AL Rookie of the Year Award by a large margin over teammate Mark Langston and Kirby Puckett of the Minnesota Twins.

HR	RBI	AVG	SLG
25	122	.318	.563

RALPH KINER 1946

Ralph Kiner had hardly played baseball in three years when he arrived at Pirates camp in 1946. He had last played at Double-A Toronto in 1943 and barely touched a bat while flying anti-submarine missions in the Navy during World War II.

But he reported to Spring Training in 1946 having added 20 pounds of muscle to his 6-foot-2 frame and began crushing the ball, winning the club's left-field job. The power display continued all season, as he became the first rookie to win a home run crown since Braggo Roth captured the 1915 American League title with seven blasts during the Deadball Era.

Kiner touched St. Louis ace Howie Pollet for his first career home run on April 18. Even though he batted just .247 and struck out a league-high 109 times — the only time he exceeded 100 punchouts in a season during his 10-year Hall-of-Fame career — he led the NL in home runs with 23.

HR	RBI	AVG	SLG
23	81	.247	.430

The mark tied a Pirates club record set by Johnny Rizzo in 1938. Although Kiner claimed that his 1946 home run crown was a fluke, he would hit a whopping 51 the following season.

Major League Baseball did not begin awarding a Rookie of the Year honor until 1947. *The Sporting News*, however, named Philadelphia outfielder Del Ennis its top first-year player, even though Ennis finished with fewer home runs and RBI than Kiner. Ennis did lead NL rookies in batting, slugging, runs, hits and doubles.

Kiner's 23 home runs as a rookie foreshadowed the rest of his career. It was the first of seven consecutive NL home run crowns for one of the most underrated power hitters in the history of the game.

WALLY BERGER 1930

Wally Berger had already endured three seasons in the Minors and was 24 years old heading into the 1930 season, wondering when he would finally get a chance in the Majors like his high school teammate Joe Cronin.

After hitting 40 homers in the Pacific Coast League in 1929, he began attracting attention from several Big League clubs. Berger, under the Cubs' control, was traded to the Boston Braves.

Tall and lanky, the outfielder swatted 38 homers as a rookie in 1930 to establish a record that stood for 57 years. A right-handed batter, he also hit .310 with 119 RBI to begin an underrated 11-year career highlighted by four All-Star selections.

Berger's rookie mark was matched by the Cincinnati Reds' Frank Robinson in 1956 and later surpassed by the Oakland A's Mark McGwire, who hit 49 home runs in 1987.

Berger

HR	RBI	AVG	SLG
38	119	.310	.614

After hitting 40 home runs in the Pacific Coast League in 1929, he began attracting attention from several Big League clubs. Berger, under the Cubs' control, was traded to the Boston Braves.

DALE ALEXANDER 1929

At 6 foot 3 and 210 pounds, Dale "Moose" Alexander loomed large as a rookie for the Detroit Tigers in 1929. Alexander had won the Triple Crown the previous season in the International League. The hulking first baseman batted .343, led the AL with 215 hits, scored 110 runs, and finished second to Al Simmons with 83 extra-base hits. He also finished among the top five in total bases, RBI, home runs, slugging, doubles and triples.

HR	RBI	AVG	SLG
25	137	.343	.580

Alexander's 137 RBI is the fourth-highest output by a rookie. He drove in six runs on Aug. 7 when he collected a home run, two doubles and a single in the Tigers' win at Cleveland. Alexander, whose career would be cut short by a leg injury, is one of just five rookies in history to amass 200-plus hits and more than 100 RBI. He's also one of a dozen players to score 100 runs in his rookie season and never again reach that figure.

MARK McGWIRE 1987

After hitting .189 during a brief call-up in 1986, Mark McGwire was no lock for the Oakland Athletics' roster coming out of Spring Training in 1987.

At 6 foot 5 and 225 pounds, the boyish, freckle-faced McGwire stood in contrast to his larger-than-life teammate and fellow "Bash Brother," Jose Canseco, who had won the Rookie of the Year Award the previous season. The 23-year-old McGwire almost seemed *svelte* in comparison.

McGwire could not read the Big E on an eye chart without contact lenses. A shy man, he preferred golf as a kid and never viewed himself as an exceptional athlete, even after starring at the University of Southern California and on the 1984 U.S. Olympic baseball team.

"I was just a basic athlete, nothing extraordinary," he said. "But I was a hard worker. And I liked to do a lot of that work where people couldn't see me."

But in 1987, he was on a national stage. He set an all-time rookie record by hitting 49 home runs, shattering the old mark of 38, shared by Wally Berger and Frank Robinson. He drove in 118 runs, batted .289 and had the highest slugging percentage (.618) in the Majors.

McGwire became just the second ballplayer, after Carlton Fisk in 1972, to be chosen unanimously as American League Rookie of the Year. No AL player had hit more home runs in a season since Roger Maris slugged 61 in 1961.

"I'm realistic," McGwire said after the season. "I don't know that I'll ever hit 49 home runs again."

In fact, he would accomplish that feat four more times.

HR	RBI	AVG	SLG
49	118	.289	.618

BLASTING ONTO THE SCENE

TOP ROOKIE HOME RUN TOTALS		
PLAYER	HR	YEAR
Mark McGwire	49	1987
Wally Berger	38	1930
Frank Robinson	38	1956
Al Rosen	37	1950
Albert Pujols	37	2001
Hal Trosky	35	1934
Rudy York	35	1937
Ron Kittle	35	1983
Mike Piazza	35	1993
Ryan Braun	**34**	**2007**

HR	RBI	AVG	SLG
34	97	.324	.634

RYAN BRAUN 2007

During his standout college career at the University of Miami, Ryan Braun often would see superstar Alex Rodriguez working out in the school weight room during the offseason.

Braun would pick the brain of the Florida resident and Major League slugger, looking for any advice that might help him on his own path to the Big Leagues.

A converted shortstop playing just his second full season at third base, Braun was sent to Triple-A near the end of Spring Training in 2007 after struggling defensively. By season's end, there was talk of him moving to the outfield, which would happen the following season. As for his offensive production, there were no complaints.

The fifth overall pick in the 2005 draft, Braun made an A-Rod–like ascension to the Major Leagues, being called up by the Brewers on May 24, 2007. Playing the next day in front of 100 friends and family in San Diego, not far from his childhood home outside Los Angeles, he doubled in his first game and homered in his second contest.

Braun didn't stop mashing. He batted .324 for the season and led NL rookies with 34 home runs. He slugged an NL-leading .634, breaking the Major League rookie record set by Mark McGwire, who slugged .618 for Oakland in 1987. Braun drove in 97 runs and added 15 stolen bases on the year.

Although Braun spent almost the entire first two months of the season in the Minors, he narrowly edged Colorado's Troy Tulowitzki to become Milwaukee's first Rookie of the Year since shortstop Pat Listach won the AL honor in 1992.

"You don't like to put expectations on players," said Brewers General Manager Doug Melvin. "But he certainly went well beyond what we anticipated from him in his first year."

chapter 8
MOUND PRESENCE

It generally takes years for even the most highly regarded pitching prospects to develop into aces. Those thrust into a prominent role at a young age usually take a few steps back before entrenching themselves in the Majors. Some need time in the Minors, learning to master their pitches, before they can dominate. Then there are the rare few that look like poised veterans from the moment they step on the mound. Some, like 19th-century standout Kid Nichols, racked up eye-popping numbers. More recently, Bob Welch's showdown with Reggie Jackson in the 1978 World Series and Kerry Wood's 20-strikeout effort have proven that rookie pitchers can provide no shortage of memorable moments.

KERRY WOOD 1998

On May 6, 1998, Kerry Wood began the game by throwing a fastball to Astros leadoff man Craig Biggio. The offering sailed over the head of Cubs catcher Sandy Martinez and plunked plate umpire Jerry Meals in the mask. It wasn't the most auspicious start, but the 20-year-old flamethrower from Texas settled down to strike out the Astros' six-time All-Star.

Mixing nasty fastballs with curves and sliders that darted in every direction, the rookie right-hander, in just his fifth Major League game, also struck out the next four batters he faced at Wrigley Field. He would strike out the side four times, finishing with 20 K's on the day. The only hit he allowed was a lucky infield ball by Ricky Gutierrez that nicked the glove of Cubs third baseman Kevin Orie and could have been scored an error. Just one other batter reached base, and that was when Biggio was hit by a pitch in the sixth.

W	L	ERA	K
13	6	3.40	233

Wood broke numerous team and rookie strikeout records that day, among them the NL single-game record (previously 19) and the rookie benchmark of 18.

"It was one of those games where everything you throw was crossing the plate," Wood said. "I was focused, though, so I had no idea how many guys I was striking out."

In his next start, on May 11, Wood fanned 13, amassing 33 K's over consecutive starts. On Aug. 26, he struck out 16. A sprained elbow ligament caused him to miss September, a harbinger of things to come, but Wood still held hitters to a league-low .196 average. He finished the year with a 13-6 record, and led the Cubs to their first postseason appearance since 1989.

The NL Rookie of the Year, Wood set a Big League record by averaging 12.58 strikeouts per nine innings. The mark has since been eclipsed but still ranks first among rookies.

MOUND PRESENCE

STEVE ROGERS 1973

Notoriously hard on himself, even as a young pitcher, Steve Rogers would throw his hands up in disgust after a bad pitch, talk to himself, glare and grimace, all the while imploring himself to do better.

The fourth overall pick in the 1971 draft, Rogers arrived in the Majors with the Montreal Expos on July 18, 1973, and proceeded to enjoy perhaps the greatest abbreviated rookie season ever. The 23-year-old right-hander pitched shutouts in his second and third starts, one of which was a one-hitter against the Phillies. He finished the season 10-5 with a minuscule 1.54 ERA over 134 innings. Walking just 49 batters and allowing a measly 93 hits, he posted an impressive WHIP of 1.06. Pitching less than half a season, he led the Expos' staff with three shutouts.

"He pitched the greatest two months of baseball in my experience," said Expos Manager Gene Mauch. "He pitched 17 consecutive powerful games."

A lean 6 foot 1, Rogers brought a deep repertoire to the mound. He threw a darting fastball, slider, a curveball at two speeds and a straight change-up.

"He has six quality pitches," Mauch said. "He has confidence he can throw all of them over the plate. And unlike most young pitchers, I've never seen him beat himself — walk a few batters in a row or make an error. He's got it all together right now."

Rogers also set an unusual record: most wins by a starter with a sub-2.00 ERA pitching fewer than 140 innings. Houston's J.R. Richard, pitching in his final season before suffering a career-ending stroke, tied the mark in 1980. Cal Eldred, a rookie with the Brewers in 1992, broke the record.

W	L	ERA	IP
10	5	1.54	134

Radatz

DICK RADATZ 1962

At 6 foot 5 and 235 pounds, Dick Radatz was nicknamed "The Monster." As a rookie in 1962, he quickly established a reputation for endurance. He led the AL with 62 appearances, while striking out 144 hitters and posting a 2.24 ERA. He saved a rookie-record 24 games, winning *The Sporting News* AL Fireman of the Year Award and finishing tied for third in the AL Rookie of the Year voting.

W	L	ERA	SV
9	6	2.24	24

"When you compare him to other guys, they couldn't do what he did," said teammate Bill Monbouquette. "Three innings one day, maybe four the next, one the next day, and three more the next. Relievers today throw one inning. Dick almost never pitched just an inning."

BOB WELCH 1978

The Dodgers' first-round pick in the 1977 draft rose quickly to the Majors. Right-hander Bob Welch made his Big League debut in June 1978, pitching two score-less frames out of the bullpen against the Astros. He notched his first save a few days later, topped the Reds in his first start the week after that, and then shut out the Giants on Aug. 5 in a pivotal NL West clash. The Giants were leading the Dodgers by 4.5 games when Welch and his nasty split-finger fastball stopped them.

The 21-year-old finished the regular season 7-4 with a 2.02 ERA in 23 games, including 13 starts. His postseason work that year would produce perhaps the most memorable moment of a career that included two All-Star selections, two world championships and 211 wins, including a 27-win Cy Young campaign in 1990.

In Game 2 of the World Series against the Yankees, the Dodgers were leading, 4-3, with one out in the top of the ninth. New York had runners on first and second. Welch was cheered wildly when he emerged from the bullpen, having become a fan favorite at Dodger Stadium in just four months. He made quick work of Yankees captain Thurman Munson, inducing a fly ball to right field, before facing Mr. October himself, Reggie Jackson.

The rookie and the veteran slugger faced off in an epic nine-pitch, six-minute clash before Jackson struck out on a high fastball, giving the Dodgers the win and Welch a save.

"I got beat, that's all," Jackson said. "I was looking for a ball I could handle, and I never got one. I wanted him to make a mistake, but he didn't."

W	L	ERA	IP
7	4	2.02	111.1

Nichols
(middle row,
far left)

PRE-1900 ROOKIES TO LEAD LEAGUE IN SHUTOUTS		
PLAYER	SHO	YEAR
George Derby	9	1881
Ben Sanders	8	1888
Kid Nichols	**7**	**1890**
Wiley Piatt	6	1895
Bill Hoffer	4	1895

KID NICHOLS 1890

Charles Augustus "Kid" Nichols accomplished more at a younger age than perhaps any pitcher in baseball history. As a 20-year-old rookie for the Boston Beaneaters in 1890, he went 27-19 with a Major League–leading seven shutouts. In 48 games that season, he threw a staggering 424 innings, striking out 222 batters and walking just 112. A superstar from the outset, Nichols took over a leadership role on a pitching staff already headlined by Hall of Famer John Clarkson.

W	L	ERA	IP
27	19	2.23	424

The Wisconsin native got off to a slow start, but boosted his record to 3-6 by tossing his first career shutout on May 21, nipping Cleveland, 1-0, in 10 innings. His 27 wins were one shy of the rookie high for 1890; Billy Rhines of Cincinnati won 28.

Nichols' rookie campaign began a streak of 10 consecutive 20-plus-win seasons, including seven years of 30 or more. He is the youngest pitcher to win 300 games, having reached that milestone during the 1900 season at the age of 30.

LARRY CORCORAN 1880

Larry Corcoran owns one of baseball's most untouchable records: a rookie-best 43 wins. Pitching for Manager Cap Anson's Chicago White Stockings in 1880, the right-hander became the first rookie ace in National League history.

W	L	ERA	IP
43	14	1.95	536.1

Corcoran made his Big League debut on May 1, beating Cincinnati on Opening Day. On July 13, he shut out the Cleveland Blues, 3-0, to post his 13th straight win and establish a new rookie record for consecutive wins. On Aug. 19, shortly after his 21st birthday, he threw his first no-hitter, defeating Boston, 6-0. It was the first of his three career no-hitters, a record for a 19th-century pitcher. Corcoran led the league in strikeouts (268) and finished second in wins. He won 170 games in his first five seasons.

ROY OSWALT 2001

The Houston Astros have traditionally flown low on the baseball radar. Overshadowed by football in Texas and without a World Series appearance through 2000, they welcomed Roy Oswalt to the Majors amid little fanfare in 2001.

The unassuming Oswalt was drafted by the Astros in the 23rd round out of tiny Holmes Community College in Goodman, Miss., in 1996. Called up to the Majors in May 2001, Oswalt made eight relief appearances before starting his first game on June 2, beating the Dodgers, 2-1. With a mid-90s fastball, sharp curveball and slight build, he was compared to Greg Maddux with harder stuff.

Oswalt went 4-0 with a 1.99 ERA in August and finished the year 14-3, breaking Houston's rookie victory record. He placed second to Albert Pujols in NL Rookie of the Year voting.

Pitching 141.2 innings, Oswalt struck out 144 batters and walked just 24. Not since 1884 had a pitcher posted a strike-out-to-walk ratio of 6:1 over more than 100 innings. Oswalt gave batters fits with his uncanny ability to change speeds.

"People would tell me my curveball was too slow — it's 20 to 22 miles per hour slower than my fastball — but I think it's a big advantage that I can add and subtract [speed] on all my pitches," Oswalt said. "No matter how hard you throw, Big League hitters are going to catch up to it."

W	L	ERA	IP
14	3	2.73	141.2

chapter 9

FAST TRACK

Unlike professional athletes in other sports, baseball players are typically unable to transition from high school or college directly to the highest level. Players usually need time in the Minors to polish their skills. There are exceptions, of course. Whether because of talent or necessity, some players make the leap and never look back. Teenager Al Kaline vaulted from his high school team to the Detroit Tigers and immediately thrived. Bob Horner may have benefited from some Minor League seasoning, but the 1978 Braves needed help immediately. Whatever the reason, the player who never sees time in the Minors is one of baseball's rarest commodities.

DAVE WINFIELD 1973

At 6 foot 6, Dave Winfield was a larger-than-life figure from the moment he debuted for San Diego on June 19, 1973, just 12 days after the Padres selected him with the fourth pick in baseball's First-Year Player Draft. A pitcher and outfielder on the University of Minnesota baseball team and a top rebounder for the Golden Gophers basketball squad, Winfield was also drafted by the Atlanta Hawks of the NBA and the Utah Stars of the ABA. Even though he didn't play college football, the Minnesota Vikings selected him in the 17th round of the NFL draft, making him the first collegiate athlete drafted by each of these major sports leagues.

A five-tool talent, Winfield hit for power and average, standing away from the plate in order to extend his long arms. Still, his best highlight-reel material came in the outfield, where he unleashed a cannon of an arm and reached over outfield walls to snare would-be homers. Playing in a pre–cable TV era —

HR	RBI	AVG	SLG
3	12	.277	.383

when West Coast boxscores often didn't appear in papers in much of the country and the nightly news programs in most cities included highlights of just the home team — Winfield was not well known outside of San Diego.

Winfield batted .273 with three homers and 12 RBI in 141 at-bats as a rookie, while clad in the garish brown and yellow uniforms that matched the McDonald's gear worn by the employees of Padres owner (and McDonald's founder) Ray Kroc. The five-year-old expansion club, managed by Don Zimmer, lost 102 games and had little reason to send its budding star to the Minors.

"The Padres started me off pinch-hitting against left-handers," Winfield recalled of the beginning of his Hall-of-Fame career. "But by the end of that year I hit better off righties. They planned to send me to the Minors the next spring, but there was just no way."

LARRY DOBY 1948

Like many players in the Negro Leagues, Larry Doby had the talent to play in the Majors much earlier than he had the opportunity. A star of the Newark Eagles from 1942–47 — before and after military service — Doby batted .341 in 1946.

The left-handed hitting second baseman caught the attention of Bill Veeck, the Cleveland Indians' owner, who was intent on joining Dodgers General Manger Branch Rickey in breaking baseball's color barrier.

Three months after Jackie Robinson's debut with Rickey's Brooklyn Dodgers, the American League was integrated when Doby stepped to the plate for Cleveland on July 5, 1947, as a pinch-hitter against Earl Harrist of the White Sox. Although Doby suffered the same discrimination and backlash that Robinson did, he received less credit as a pioneer.

"The only difference was that Jackie Robinson got all the publicity," Doby later said. "You didn't hear much about what I was going through because the media didn't want to repeat the same story."

HR	RBI	AVG	OBP
14	66	.301	.384

Doby played only briefly in 1947, but assumed a full-time role the following season, batting .301 for the pennant-winning Indians. He hit .318 in the Tribe's six-game World Series victory over the Boston Braves, providing a single, double and an RBI in Game 2. In Game 4, he delivered a 400-foot home run off Boston's Johnny Sain.

The home run capped Doby's rookie season in more ways than one.

"I hit a home run off Johnny Sain to help Steve Gromek win, and in the clubhouse the photographers took a picture of Gromek and me hugging," Doby told Dave Anderson of *The New York Times* in 1987. "That picture went all over the country. I think it was one of the first, if not *the* first, [images] of a black guy and a white guy hugging, just happy because they won a ballgame."

DOBY'S 1948 WORLD SERIES STATS							
H	R	HR	RBI	BB	AVG	OBP	SLG
7	1	1	2	2	.318	.375	.500

DOBY'S JERSEY

BOB HORNER 1978

So desperate were the Atlanta Braves for power and help at third base in 1978 that they scrapped plans to start No. 1 overall draft pick Bob Horner at Double-A and brought him directly to the Majors. Just 10 days after playing his final game for Arizona State, the ink barely dry on a contract that included a $175,000 signing bonus, Horner smacked a home run off the Pirates' Bert Blyleven in his first professional game.

Burly with curly blonde hair, the thick-necked slugger drew comparisons to Harmon Killebrew. Horner played mostly second base and shortstop in college but lined up exclusively at third base as a rookie. Although he missed the first two months of the 1978 season and played in just 89 games, he belted 23 home runs in 323 at-bats and won the NL Rookie of the Year Award by a comfortable margin over San Diego's Ozzie Smith.

HR	RBI	AVG	SLG
23	63	.266	.539

Horner's 23 home runs are the most ever by a rookie who played in fewer than 100 games. He not only led all rookies in homers, but also ranked eighth in the NL in at-bats per home run, with a longball every 14.043 at-bats.

With promising rookie catcher Dale Murphy on the roster as well, the hapless Braves suddenly had hope for the future. "Nobody has ever come straight into the Majors and done what he has done," Braves Owner Ted Turner said of Horner.

Horner was ready for the challenge the Big Leagues had to offer. "I knew that when I got to the Majors, I would want to stay," he said. "I didn't want to have all my hopes shattered like one of those David Clydes — stay a year and then go down."

EDDIE PLANK 1901

Eddie Plank fidgeted on the mound, talked to himself before every pitch and slowed the pace of the game. His antics frustrated teammates, opponents and fans, but nobody could argue with the methods that would produce baseball's first left-handed 300-game winner. Besides his unique mound routine, he threw with an odd "cross-fire" motion, hurling across his body. The idiosyncratic wind-up resulted in wildness at first — he led the league with 13 wild pitches as a rookie — but he worked diligently and eventually became known for his control.

W	L	ERA	IP
17	13	3.31	260.2

Having pitched for Gettysburg College while enrolled at the Gettysburg Academy prep school, Plank joined the Philadelphia Athletics in 1901. As a rookie, Plank went 17-13 with a 3.31 ERA and 28 complete games. He combined with Snake Wiltse (13-5) to give the Athletics the second-winningest pair of rookie left-handers in baseball history.

TED LYONS 1924

Ted Lyons, a star second baseman growing up in Vinton, La., enrolled at Baylor University with plans to become a lawyer. He joined the Baylor baseball team, but was moved to the pitcher's mound because of the team's surplus of infielders. He was so effective toeing the rubber that he caught the attention of several Major League clubs and changed his career plans.

Lyons signed with the White Sox after Owner Charles Comiskey promised him that he would not be demoted to the Minors until he had spent

W	L	ERA	IP
12	11	4.87	216.1

at least one full year in the Majors. Lyons appeared in just nine games in 1923, and then went 12-11 with a 4.87 ERA as a rookie in 1924. Although not especially impressive, Lyons was one of the better pitchers on the last-place White Sox. He would play his entire 21-year career with the South Siders and become a fan favorite. Lyons led the league in wins (21) and shutouts (5) in his sophomore campaign, and he tossed a no-hitter in 1926.

AL KALINE 1954

Detroit Tigers scout Ed Katalinas discovered 15-year-old Al Kaline while scouting another Baltimore schoolboy talent in 1950.

"He was shy, always had been," Katalinas told *Sports Illustrated* six years later. "But there was no doubt about what he wanted to do. He wanted to play baseball, period."

Kaline hit .609 in American Legion Ball in 1951 and was a perennial selection to the All-Maryland team while starring at Baltimore's Southern High. By the end of his senior year, every Big League club was pursuing him; the Phillies and Cardinals were particularly smitten with the prospect.

Kaline signed with the Tigers on June 19, 1953, and made his Major League debut six days later, barely six months after his 18th birthday. He played sparingly during the remainder of the '53 season but became a full-time player the following year at 19. Although his fielding, throwing and baserunning were

HR	RBI	AVG	H
4	43	.276	139

already considered exceptional, his rookie numbers at the plate were modest: a .276 average with four home runs and 43 RBI.

One of just five teenage rookies since World War II to play at least 100 games, Kaline also produced one of the more puzzling stats: fewest runs scored by an outfielder with 500 or more at-bats. By walking just 22 times and posting a .305 OBP — both of which would be career lows — Kaline crossed the plate just 42 times.

Although Kaline received one of the 24 votes for American League Rookie of the Year, finishing behind the Yankees' Bob Grim and Jim Finigan of the Athletics, few could have predicted his breakout sophomore campaign. In 1955, Kaline led the league in batting (.340), hits (200) and total bases (321), while belting 27 home runs and driving in 102 runs. Still just 20 years old at season's end — the youngest-ever batting champ and AL MVP runner-up (to Yogi Berra) — Kaline had established himself as a star.

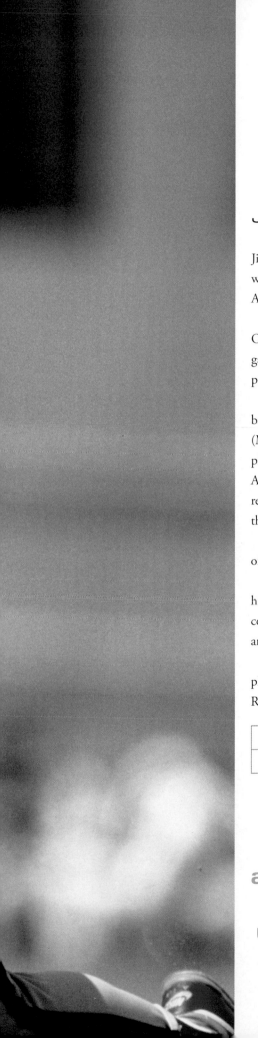

JIM ABBOTT 1989

Jim Abbott never let the lack of a right hand slow down his athletic career. So perhaps it was appropriate that he went directly from the University of Michigan to the California Angels without a stop in the Minors.

Actually, the eighth overall pick in the 1988 draft spent the summer with the U.S. Olympic team, where he pitched Team USA to a 5-3 win over Japan in the gold medal game. There was talk the following spring of sending Abbott to Double-A, but he proved he was ready for the Majors.

Born with only a nub where his right hand would be, he gravitated toward baseball even though his parents hoped he would pursue soccer. Also a quarterback at Flint (Mich.) Central High, Abbott batted .427 during his final high school baseball season, playing first base and left field when he wasn't pitching. His fielding was no concern. After each pitch, he deftly slipped his glove from his right arm to his left to catch and then removed the glove to throw. The so-called "Abbott Switch" was so smooth and seamless that it was easy to forget he had just one hand.

"I've been blessed with a pretty good left arm and a not-so-great right arm," he often said.

The gregarious Abbott sometimes grew weary of the constant media queries about his handicap, but he recognized that his success provided hope to children with similar conditions. He patiently handled the interviews, answered a constant stream of mail and met numerous handicapped children at the ballpark.

Just 21 as a rookie, he posted a 12-12 record and a 3.92 ERA, throwing four complete games and two shutouts for the Angels. He finished fifth in the American League Rookie of the Year voting, proving again that he pitched at no disadvantage.

W	L	ERA	IP
12	12	3.92	181.1

He deftly slipped his glove from his right arm to his left to catch and then removed the glove to throw. The "Abbott Switch" was so smooth and seamless that it was easy to forget he had just one hand.

chapter 10

COOPERSTOWN BOUND

Sometimes you just know. Because sometimes a rookie will exhibit such awe-inspiring, polished skills that it's possible to envision what his Hall of Fame plaque might read. Early pitching stars such as John Montgomery Ward and Grover Cleveland Alexander were such talents, dominating the game seemingly from their first pitches. The National League benefited from the arrival of three such phenoms in a four-year span in the second half of the 1950s. By the time Frank Robinson, Orlando Cepeda and Willie McCovey completed their rookie campaigns, they were on their way toward Cooperstown.

FRANK ROBINSON 1956

Frank Robinson likes to recall the time when a scout told his mother that her son could sign for $3,500. "My mother said, 'That's fine, but I don't think I have $3,500.'"

The self-deprecating Robinson was a bargain at any price. At age 17, he signed with the Cincinnati Reds out of McClymonds High School in Oakland, Calif., and batted .348 in 72 Pioneer League games in 1953. After hitting .336 for Columbia of the Sally League in 1954, he was disappointed to return to A-ball the following season. Robinson finally got the call to the Majors in 1956 after beating out several veterans for the Reds' left-field job in Spring Training.

Playing for the princely sum of $6,000, Robinson dug his spikes into the batter's box, scratching the white chalk line away from the front of the box and putting his left foot almost at the edge of the plate. As a result, he was plunked a league-high 20

HR	RBI	AVG	SLG
38	83	.290	.558

times, but the routine would never change throughout his career. Robinson became the first rookie ever to hit at least 20 home runs and be hit by at least 20 pitches in the same season.

The 20-year-old Robinson doubled in his first Big League at-bat, and on April 28 he touched Cubs lefty Paul Minner for the first of his 586 career home runs. He tied Wally Berger's rookie record for most homers (38), a mark that would stand until Mark McGwire swatted 49 in 1987. Robinson, who led the National League in runs scored (122), was the unanimous selection for the NL Rookie of the Year Award, batting .290 with 83 RBI. He also finished seventh in MVP voting.

Robinson's epic rookie season helped the long-struggling Reds — who hadn't won more than 80 games since 1944 — leap into third place with 91 wins, just two games behind the pennant-winning Dodgers. The bargain outfielder was on his way to Cooperstown.

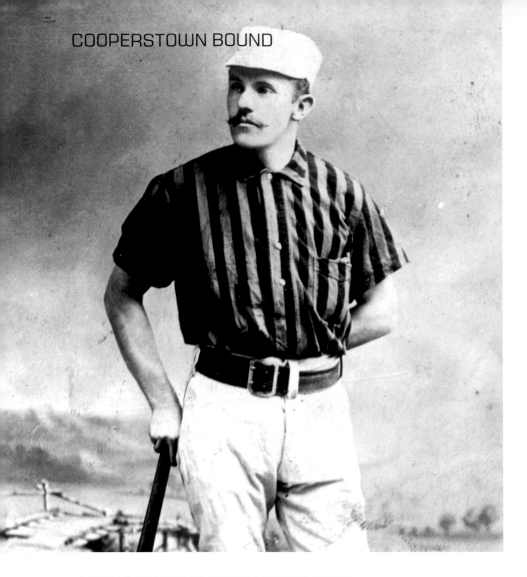

JOHN MONTGOMERY WARD 1878

A baseball pioneer, John Montgomery Ward was a star during the game's transition from club to professional sport. Born in 1860, he attended Pennsylvania State University at age 13. There he became one of the first practitioners of the curveball.

In 1878, he joined the Providence Grays of the National League. As a rookie, he won 22 games with a league-leading 1.51 ERA, while throwing 334 innings. In 1879, Ward led Providence to the pennant with a league-high 47 victories, and in 1880, he authored the second perfect game in Big League history. Arm problems forced a move to shortstop, where he would continue his Hall-of-Fame career.

A staunch opponent of the reserve

W	L	ERA	IP
22	13	1.51	334

clause, which virtually tied a player to a team in perpetuity, Ward earned a law degree from Columbia University in 1885 and organized the first players' union. Four years later, he led a player revolt that resulted in the short-lived Players League. The last line of Ward's Cooperstown plaque understates the impact Ward had on the game on and off the field. "Played important part in establishing modern organized baseball," it reads. Bryan Di Salvatore, author of the Ward biography *A Clever Base-Ballist*, is more direct. "For a strange, brief period," he wrote, "John Ward was the most important man of his profession."

ORLANDO CEPEDA 1958

Playing their first season in San Francisco, the Giants discovered a future Hall of Famer in 20-year-old Orlando Cepeda. The upbeat first baseman grew up in Santurce, Puerto Rico, where his father, Pedro "Perucho" Cepeda, was considered the greatest Puerto Rican player of his time. During the winter of 1954–55, Orlando played on the Santurce winter team with future Giants teammate Willie Mays.

As a first-year player, Cepeda drew comparisons to his great teammate. He led National League rookies in most offensive categories, including batting (.312), home runs (25), RBI (96), runs (88), slugging (.512) and OBP (.342). His league-leading 38 doubles would be a career best, and he was unanimously voted NL Rookie of the Year.

"He's the second-best 20-year-old rookie I ever saw," said San Francisco skipper Bill Rigney. "The other one was Willie Mays."

Cepeda's rookie season was not without its challenges. His teammate and close friend, veteran pitcher Ruben Gomez, helped touch off a bench-clearing brawl in Pittsburgh. Angry with Pirates Manager Danny Murtaugh, Cepeda made a move for one of his bats as the scuffle ensued. Mays tackled the "Baby Bull" before he got anywhere, but the National League still fined the rookie $100.

Cepeda was one of four Giants rookies in Rigney's regular lineup in 1958. Two others, including Felipe Alou, saw significant time in the outfield. Led by Cepeda, the rookies helped the Giants improve 11 games from the '57 season and finish third in the NL pennant race.

HR	RBI	AVG	SLG
25	96	.312	.512

WILLIE McCOVEY 1959

The San Francisco Giants faced a pleasant dilemma at the beginning of the 1959 season. With Orlando Cepeda, the reigning National League Rookie of the Year, entrenched at first base, they sent promising prospect Willie McCovey back to Triple-A Phoenix.

The 6-foot-4 slugger, known as "Stretch," had a ferocious left-handed swing and had already racked up 73 home runs in four Minor League seasons, including 14 longballs in 1958. Still just 21, he returned to the Valley of the Sun and smacked another 29 homers in 349 at-bats while hitting .372.

With the Giants battling the rival Los Angeles Dodgers and the Milwaukee Braves for the NL pennant, they moved Cepeda to the outfield in July and called up McCovey, who proceeded to enjoy perhaps the best two-month stretch of any late-season call-up in baseball history.

Facing the Phillies' Robin Roberts in his first game, McCovey went 4 for 4 with two triples. The Giants went on to win 10 of the next 12 games. McCovey hit .354 with 13 homers and 38 RBI in 52 games down the stretch, pushing the Giants within striking distance of the postseason. Yet the Giants lost seven of their final eight games to finish in third place.

Despite the short rookie tenure and some shaky defensive play at first, McCovey was the second consecutive Giants player chosen as NL Rookie of the Year by a unanimous vote. The honor came thanks in part to the fact that the Reds' Vada Pinson, who hit .316 with 20 home runs while leading the league in doubles (47) and runs (131), lost his rookie status after collecting six at-bats too many the previous season. Still, as an eligible rookie, McCovey was more than deserving of the honor.

HR	RBI	AVG	SLG
13	38	.354	.656

99

GROVER CLEVELAND ALEXANDER 1911

PAUL WANER 1926

Grover Cleveland "Pete" Alexander, born in Nebraska during the first term of United States President Grover Cleveland, emerged in 1911 just as the great Cy Young was winding down his illustrious 22-year career. It was only appropriate that Alexander's first year was Young's last, since Alexander assumed the mantel of baseball's best pitcher. On Sept. 7, 1911, the two squared off, with Alexander's Philadelphia Phillies defeating Young's Boston Rustlers, 1-0. The game was the first of four consecutive shutouts for Alexander, who as a rookie led the National League in wins (28), shutouts (seven), complete games (31) and innings pitched (367).

W	L	ERA	IP
28	13	2.57	367

Alexander's inaugural season established his reputation as a workhorse. He would lead the league in innings pitched in seven of his first 10 seasons. During that stretch, Alexander also would pace the NL in wins, strikeouts, shutouts and complete games six times apiece.

Coming off a terrific 1925 season in the Pacific Coast League, in which he batted .401 with 75 doubles, Paul Waner seemed poised to make the Pittsburgh Pirates' roster heading into Spring Training in 1926. But that goal almost didn't come to fruition for the future "Big Poison." Waner hit poorly that spring, and even when he made the roster, the Pirates had veteran first baseman Stuffy McInnis teach him a different position, which he would play on occasion in ensuing seasons.

HR	RBI	AVG	OBP
8	79	.336	.413

As a rookie, Waner was part of a future Hall-of-Fame outfield with Kiki Cuyler and Max Carey, at least until Carey was claimed off waivers by Brooklyn late in the season.

Playing right field, the left-handed hitting Waner batted .336 and led the NL with 22 triples. One of just two National Leaguers to score 100 runs, he finished third in slugging and fourth in total bases. On Aug. 26 against the Giants, he went 6 for 6 with three singles, two doubles and a triple.

EDDIE MURRAY 1977

As a newcomer in 1977, Eddie Murray was uncomfortable with attention from media and fans, including the chants of "Ed-die, Ed-die" that he ultimately would hear throughout his career.

"When you come out of the Minors and get into a Major League uniform and all of a sudden hear that, it's awesome," Murray said during his 2003 Hall of Fame induction, recalling his touted rookie debut. "It made me uncomfortable, but I learned to deal with it so I could go out and do my job."

Just 21 as a rookie in Baltimore, Murray had Gold Glove–caliber talent at first base and, indeed, would win the award three times from 1982–84. But Manager Earl Weaver used the switch-hitter mostly as a DH, partly to ease the transition to the Bigs and partly because veteran Lee May was still effective at first.

With the Seattle Mariners and Toronto Blue Jays joining the American League in '77, offensive numbers boomed throughout the game. Murray and Seattle's Ruppert Jones played the most games (160) among rookies. Murray also smashed 27 home runs and had 88 RBI for an Orioles team that finished with 97 wins.

Murray set an Orioles rookie record with 611 at-bats. On Aug. 3, facing the A's in Oakland, he went deep from each side of the plate — the first of a record-11 times he would do so. Murray won the AL Rookie of the Year Award by a narrow margin over Mitchell Page of the A's, the start of a long, consistent career for "Steady Eddie."

HR	RBI	AVG	SLG
27	88	.283	.470

MOST REGULAR-SEASON GAMES PLAYED BY A ROOKIE

PLAYER	GAMES	YEAR
Hideki Matsui	163	2003
Dick Allen	162	1964
Johnny Ray	162	1982
Jeff Conine	162	1993
Albert Pujols	161	2001
Ken Hubbs	160	1962
Tommie Agee	160	1966
Pedro Garcia	160	1973
Ruppert Jones	160	1977
Eddie Murray	**160**	**1977**

TED WILLIAMS 1939

It was before his rookie season in 1939 when Ted Williams uttered his most famous quote. Speaking to a group of sportswriters, he said "All I want out of life is that when I walk down the street, folks will say, 'There goes the greatest hitter who ever lived.'"

It didn't take long for that goal to look like a realistic prospect. Brash and rail-thin with a beautiful left-handed swing resembling that of "Shoeless" Joe Jackson, Williams wielded a light bat that produced tremendous speed.

In his autobiography, *My Turn at Bat*, Williams recalled his first Spring Training, portraying himself as "a nuisance to everybody, asking questions about hitting, asking about this pitcher or that one, quizzing every player on the team."

Mentored by Hall of Famer Rogers Hornsby while in the Minor Leagues, Williams brought a swagger to the Majors unlike any rookie before, or maybe even since. The 20-year-old referred to himself in the

HR	RBI	AVG	SLG
31	145	.327	.609

third person as "The Kid," and since he forever displayed boyish enthusiasm regarding the game and hitting, the nickname stuck for the rest of his life.

Playing right field for the only season in his career, Williams rankled teammates with his indifference toward working to improve defensively. But there was no arguing with his work ethic at the plate.

On April 23, he smacked his first career home run, part of a four-hit day. After April, he never had fewer than 22 RBI in any month. For the season, he batted .327 with 44 doubles, 11 triples and 31 home runs. He walked 107 times and led the American League in both total bases (344) and RBI (145).

Although Williams famously feuded with fans and media later in his career, his rookie season was relatively free of conflict. "I can't imagine anyone having a better, happier first year in the Big Leagues," he said years later.

WILLIAMS' BAT

chapter 11

BEST PROSPECTS EVER

There may be no such thing as a can't-miss prospect. Baseball's First-Year Player Draft is replete with cautionary tales. No. 1 picks such as Danny Goodwin and Matt Anderson are among the many who flamed out; in 1978, the Royals' Clint Hurdle was billed as the second coming of George Brett. Throughout the 1980s, several Mets prospects were touted as the next big things. Some, like Darryl Strawberry and Dwight Gooden, lived up to the hype. Others, like Gregg Jefferies and David West, not so much. Then there are players like George Sisler, Joe DiMaggio and Mickey Mantle, who exceeded even their lofty advance billings.

GEORGE SISLER 1915

George Sisler, a University of Michigan graduate with a degree in mechanical engineering, was one of the most versatile baseball players of his era. After a previous contract signed when he was a minor was declared null and void, Sisler signed with the St. Louis Browns in 1915.

The Browns hired his former college coach, Branch Rickey, as manager and were ready to give Sisler — who liked the idea of going straight to the Majors — a chance to contribute immediately. Like fellow rookie Babe Ruth, he was a dual threat on the mound and at the plate.

As a rookie, the left-hander went 4-4 with a 2.83 ERA in 15 games, including eight starts. On Aug. 2, he lost to his idol, Walter Johnson, but came back to beat "The Big Train," 2-1, on Aug. 29. *The Washington Post* labeled him a "baseball freak," referring to Sisler's hitting, pitching and fielding prowess.

Sisler, for his part, was still a wide-eyed rookie, especially after beating Johnson, which even years later he would describe as his greatest day in baseball.

"For a minute I thought maybe I'd go over and shake his hand and tell him that I was sorry I beat him," he said. "But I guess that was just the silly idea of a young kid who had just come face to face with his idol and beaten him."

In an era dominated by pitching, Sisler put up strong numbers at the plate during his first year, batting .285 with three homers and 29 RBI in 274 at-bats. Like Ruth, Sisler was more valuable as an everyday player than on the mound. As a rookie, "Gorgeous George" played 36 games at first base, the position where he would emerge as one of baseball's all-time greats. In 1920, Sisler would set a Major League record with 257 hits, while also batting .407, driving in 122 runs and stealing 42 bases.

HR	RBI	AVG	SLG
3	29	.285	.369

TODD VAN POPPEL 1993

A hard-throwing, 6-foot-5 right-hander from Martin High School in Arlington, Texas, Todd Van Poppel was neither the first nor the last Texas flamethrower to draw comparisons to Nolan Ryan.

In 1990, the Atlanta Braves considered making Van Poppel the top overall pick, but instead tapped Florida high schooler Chipper Jones, believing Van Poppel would accept a scholarship offer from the University of Texas if they drafted him. Twelve other teams passed before the Oakland A's drafted Van Poppel and signed him to a record $1.2 million contract, making him the first high school pitcher ever to receive a Major League deal.

Van Poppel was the first of four moundsmen Oakland drafted among the top 36 picks in 1990, a group dubbed "The Four Aces" by *Baseball America*. The A's, coming off three straight World Series appearances — including one championship — expected Van Poppel to become a part of their rotation in 1991. But he experienced control problems during Spring Training and spent most of the year at Double-A Huntsville (Ala.), where he walked 90 batters in 132.1 innings.

Van Poppel made just one Big League start in mid-September 1991, and got shelled by the White Sox. He reappeared in 1993 and went 6-6 with a 5.04 ERA in 16 starts. Unable to develop a reliable off-speed pitch and continuing to struggle with control, he led the AL with 89 walks in the strike-shortened 1994 season. Van Poppel won just 18 games in parts of five seasons with the A's before finding a niche as a journeyman middle reliever. By 2004 — at age 32 — he was out of baseball.

W	L	ERA	IP
6	6	5.04	84

Marquard

RUBE MARQUARD 1909

Richard William Marquard was no naive country "rube." He was a city kid from Cleveland, a sophisticated, teetotaler who wed Broadway actress Blossom Seeley. He earned his nickname as a Minor Leaguer because his pitching was reminiscent of that of Hall of Famer Rube Waddell.

In 1908, the New York Giants paid a record $11,000 to purchase the rights to Marquard, who had recorded 51 wins in the previous two Minor League seasons, including 28 for Indianapolis in '08. Rushed to the Majors before he was ready, the lefty struggled, going 5-13 in '09 and earning the nickname "the $11,000 lemon."

But Marquard would make lemonade. In 1911, he went 24-7, leading the NL with 237 K's and finishing seventh in MVP voting — which, at the time, encompassed both leagues. It was the first of three straight 20-win seasons; the Giants captured pennants each year.

W	L	ERA	IP
5	13	2.60	173

Rushed to the Majors before he was ready, the lefty struggled, going 5-13 in '09 and earning the nickname "the $11,000 lemon." But Marquard would make lemonade. In 1911, he went 24-7, leading the NL with 237 K's.

WILLIE KAMM 1923

A slick-fielding third baseman for the Pacific Coast League's San Francisco Seals, Willie Kamm became the first Minor League player sold for five figures when the Chicago White Sox bought his services for $10,000 in May 1922. Remaining with the Seals for the rest of the year, he hit .342.

In 1923, Kamm joined the White Sox and hit .292 with 39 doubles, the most ever for a rookie third baseman in the American League. He also knocked in 87 baserunners, good for second most on a team that was still rebounding from the 1919 Black Sox scandal.

Kamm spent 13 seasons in the Majors between the Sox and Indians. He led the AL in walks (90) in 1925 and enjoyed his best season at the plate in 1928, when he batted .308 and finished fifth in MVP voting. He led AL third basemen in fielding percentage eight times.

HR	RBI	AVG	SB
6	87	.292	18

JOE DiMAGGIO 1936

Despite being a reserved young man when he joined the New York Yankees in 1936, there was nothing quiet about Joe DiMaggio's game. Even as a rookie, the 21-year-old was well on his way to becoming a larger-than-life figure.

He had batted .361 in four seasons for the San Francisco Seals of the Pacific Coast League, including a .398 effort with 34 home runs in 1935 and a 61-game hitting streak in 1933. Lanky yet graceful in the outfield, he produced ferocious power at the plate with an effortless right-handed stroke.

At the start of his rookie season, DiMaggio missed several games with a foot injury but went 3 for 6 with a triple and three runs in his debut on May 3. On June 24 he hit a record-tying two homers in a 10-run Yankees fifth inning, driving in five runs. He also stroked two doubles in an 18-11 Yankees win over the White Sox. On July 7, at Braves Field in Boston, DiMaggio became the first-ever rookie to start in an All-Star Game.

HR	RBI	AVG	H
29	125	.323	206

It didn't take long for DiMaggio's outfield play to draw rave reviews, too. In a May game against Detroit, DiMaggio ran down a drive by Charlie Gehringer and cut down a runner trying to tag from third.

"DiMaggio, whose work afield was sparkling all afternoon, made a spectacular ninth-inning throw to home," *The New York Times* reported.

Although he played in just 138 games, DiMaggio finished in the top 10 in the American League in home runs (29), hits (206), doubles (44), triples (15), runs (132) and RBI (125), while setting Yankee rookie records in each of those categories, in addition to at-bats (637) and slugging (.576). He's one of just five rookies to collect 200-plus hits and 100-plus RBI.

ROOKIES WITH 200 HITS, 100 RBI			
PLAYER	H	RBI	YEAR
Jimmy Williams	219	116	1899
Dale Alexander	215	137	1929
Hal Trosky	206	142	1934
Joe DiMaggio	**206**	**125**	**1936**
Frank McCormick	209	106	1938

Hurdle (running)

CLINT HURDLE 1978

Clint Hurdle appeared on the cover of *Sports Illustrated* on March 20, 1978, alongside the headline "This Year's Phenom." In an accompanying article, Charlie Lau, the Kansas City Royals' hitting instructor who tutored Hall of Famer George Brett, called Hurdle "the best hitting prospect I've ever seen in our organization." John Schuerholz, the team's director of scouting and player development and a man not given to hyperbole, said, "I bubble when I think about his potential."

HR	RBI	AVG	H
7	56	.265	110

The Royals considered their 1975 first-round pick another golden boy like Brett, who predicted a .300 season for Hurdle as a rookie. Kansas City even sold veteran John Mayberry to open a position for Hurdle. Hurdle struggled at first base and eventually landed in the outfield. His rookie year was one of just two seasons in which he played more than 100 games. He made his final Big League appearance as a player at age 29, collecting just 360 career hits before finding success as manager of the Colorado Rockies.

STEPHEN STRASBURG

Stephen Strasburg's legend grew fast. Undrafted out of high school, the portly righty could barely throw 90 mph — not fast enough to impress Hall of Famer Tony Gwynn, the San Diego State baseball coach. But Gwynn took the 6-foot-4 pitcher on as a project, only to see Strasburg almost drop out of school after two weeks of training.

Thankfully he stuck with it. With the help of the Aztecs' strength coach, Strasburg transformed into a solid 220 pounds, throwing

100 mph. In 2009, the junior was regarded as the best pitching prospect in a generation, going 13-1 with a 1.32 ERA and 195 K's in 109 innings. The Nationals drafted him No. 1 overall.

"He really has no flaws," said Kevin Towers, general manager of the Padres. "You see guys throw in the high 90s, but they usually have no idea where it's going. He can throw in the high 90s comfortably and locate it."

GROVE'S GLOVE

LEFTY GROVE 1925

Lefty Grove should have been in the Major Leagues earlier. A star for the great Baltimore Orioles of the International League during the early 1920s, he pitched for Owner Jack Dunn, the same man who discovered Babe Ruth.

Grove spent five seasons in Baltimore, winning 25 or more games three times, before Dunn finally received an acceptable offer for his ace, selling him to Connie Mack's Philadelphia Athletics for a then-record $100,600.

The 25-year-old made his Major League debut on April 14, 1925, along with batterymate Mickey Cochrane, going just 3.2 innings against the Boston Red Sox. He had difficulty adjusting to the Big Leagues, and endured arm trouble in his maiden season, managing a modest 10-12 record — the only losing campaign of his career. He still led the AL with 116 strikeouts, eight more than Washington's Walter Johnson recorded. It was the first of seven consecutive seasons that he would lead the circuit in strikeouts, and the only time in his 17-year career he would post the most walks (131).

Grove began to find his groove the following season, in 1926, posting the league's lowest ERA (2.51), the first of his record nine ERA titles. He struck out 194 batters, his second-highest total for a season, and finished eighth in MVP voting. In 1927, he won 20 games for the first of what would be eight times. From 1928–31, he posted a staggering 103-23 mark, with the Athletics winning the World Series in 1929 and '30. His 1931 season, in which he went 31-4 with a 2.06 ERA, is considered among the greatest pitching efforts of all time.

W	L	ERA	K
10	12	4.75	116

WILLIE MAYS 1951

As a teen in Alabama, Willie Mays caught the eye of many Big League teams. A Boston Braves scout recommended signing him, but the team declined, depriving Braves fans of a potential Mays–Hank Aaron outfield. Instead, the scout tipped off a colleague with the New York Giants.

Mays was batting .477 in Double-A when he got the call to the Majors in 1951. Just two weeks beyond his 20th birthday, he made his Big League debut on May 25 in Philadelphia and began his career in a 0-for-12 slump. Mays initially was intimidated by Manager Leo Durocher, but the skipper eventually set the youngster's mind at ease.

"I wanted to quit," Mays recalled. "I was 0 for 12, and when nobody was looking I cried a lot. Then Leo told me that even if I batted .100, I was his center fielder. He told me there was no way he was going to send me back to the Minors."

The next day, Mays homered off the Braves' Warren Spahn at the Polo Grounds. Mays played a key role in the Giants' late-season comeback against the Dodgers, making spectacular plays in center field and overcoming his slow start at the plate to win NL Rookie of the Year honors by a wide margin. That year, he batted .274 with 20 home runs and 68 RBI.

Mays ended the regular season in the on-deck circle when Bobby Thomson hit "The Shot Heard 'Round the World" off the Dodgers' Ralph Branca, sending the Giants to the World Series, where he managed just four hits in 22 at-bats during the six-game loss to the Yankees.

Drafted by the U.S. Army in 1952, Mays missed most of that season and all of 1953 before returning for an MVP year in 1954.

HR	RBI	AVG	SLG
20	68	.274	.472

BRIEN TAYLOR

A 6-foot-4 lefty who fired off baseballs like rockets from a bazooka, Brien Taylor was considered the best high school pitching prospect ever when he became available for the 1991 amateur draft at age 19. As a senior at North Carolina's East Carteret High, Taylor struck out 213 hitters and walked just 28 over 88 innings. His fastball topped out at 99 mph and his curveball showed promise.

The Yankees, coming off a 95-loss season, selected Taylor with the first overall pick in the draft. Working with agent Scott Boras, he leveraged the threat of enrolling in college into a $1.55 million bonus, by far an amateur-player record. Boras, who has represented players for three decades, said, "Brien Taylor, to this day, is the best high school pitcher I've seen."

Taylor thrived in Class-A, striking out 187 in 1992. *Baseball America* named him the game's best prospect that year. In 1993, he had a 3.48 ERA in Double-A. But on Dec. 18, 1993, Taylor got in a fight in a North Carolina trailer park, tearing the labrum in his pitching shoulder, effectively ending his career. He never advanced past Double-A, and retired in 2000.

MANTLE'S BAT

MICKEY MANTLE 1951

Mickey Mantle was just 19 when he began his first year in the Bigs with the Yankees in 1951, but after struggling to make contact at the plate, he spent six weeks in the Minors in Kansas City, Mo. A switch-hitting slugger with speed, the Oklahoma native was painfully shy as a rookie, struggling in the New York spotlight and feeling the pressure of following in a long line of Yankee greats.

"I was scared," Mantle later recalled. "People forget when I first came to the Yankees that Casey Stengel said I was going to be the next Babe Ruth, Lou Gehrig and Joe DiMaggio rolled into one."

HR	RBI	AVG	SLG
13	65	.267	.443

After returning from the Minors that summer, he ended the '51 season batting .267 with 13 homers and 65 RBI in 96 games. Mantle was promised $7,500 for the season if he stuck with the team after June 15. Even though he was sent down in May, he received the entire sum. He also got the first of his 59 career World Series hits in the Yankees' win over the Giants.

chapter 12

NO. 1 PICKS

Not every No.1 pick from the First-Year Player Draft becomes a star. For every Ken Griffey Jr. who matures into a full-fledged superstar, there is a David Clyde or Kris Benson who never distinguishes himself. For every Joe Mauer, there is a Danny Goodwin or Shawn Abner. Beginning in 1965, the First-Year Player Draft has been a crucial pipeline for talent entering the Major Leagues. Some top selections, like Alex Rodriguez and Chipper Jones, live up to their advanced billing, developing into the finished products that scouts envisioned them to be when they were 18 years old. Many more, like Pat Burrell, Andy Benes and Darin Erstad, become solid contributors, though not all-time greats.

ALEX RODRIGUEZ 1995

The 1995 Seattle Mariners had a backlog of veteran middle infielders in players like Joey Cora, Felix Fermin and Luis Sojo. The makeup of the roster meant that the player soon to be known simply as "A-Rod" spent much of the season in the Minors before being called up in July.

HR	RBI	AVG	SLG
5	19	.232	.408

The enduring image from Alex Rodriguez's rookie season is of the 20-year-old consoling a weeping Cora in the dugout following the final out of the ALCS, when the Indians ended the Mariners' remarkable "Refuse to Lose" season.

Rodriguez made his Big League debut on July 7, 1994, becoming the first 18-year-old to play in the Majors in a decade, and only the third shortstop since 1900. In 48 games with Seattle in '95, he batted just .232 with five homers and 19 RBI.

At 6 foot 3, the No. 1 overall pick in the 1993 draft still showed signs of fulfilling the awesome potential he displayed at Westminster Christian High School in Miami. Born in New York City, his family moved to the Dominican Republic when he was 4 years old. They returned to the United States four years later, settling in Miami. Rodriguez's father, Victor, left the family, and his mother, Lourdes, worked two jobs to put him through private school. He grew up with a poster of Cal Ripken Jr. above his bed and wore No. 3 in deference to Dale Murphy, the former Atlanta Braves slugger he watched frequently on TBS.

As a rookie, Rodriguez was viewed as the leader of the next group of big, power-hitting shortstops who, like Ripken, would redefine the position.

"I can't be compared to Cal," Rodriguez said at the time. "When I was 10 years old, he already had five years in the Big Leagues. But he's the type of player I'd like to be — a classy guy who plays hard every day and gives back to his community."

JOSH HAMILTON 2007

With the first pick in the 1999 First-Year Player Draft, Tampa Bay's front office knew it would pick a Josh, and the club eventually chose slugging outfielder Josh Hamilton over flame-throwing right-hander Josh Beckett. Pre-draft stories referred to Hamilton as "The Natural," and the Rays believed he had a higher upside than Beckett.

"In scouting, like any other business, when you see something special, that heart goes pitter-patter," said then–Tampa Bay GM Chuck LaMar.

At 6 foot 4, wearing size 19 shoes, Hamilton displayed awesome power, manners and a work ethic that impressed the organization, which envisioned the 18-year-old in its Major League lineup by 2003. That season, Beckett led the Florida Marlins to a World Series title. Hamilton, meanwhile, was addicted to drugs and in a downward spiral that kept him out of baseball for the greater part of four seasons. So far had Hamilton fallen that Tampa Bay, mired in the bottom of the American League East, left him unprotected before the Rule 5 Draft in 2006, thinking no one would want the troubled player.

HR	RBI	AVG	SLG
19	47	.292	.554

During his exile, Hamilton trained in Clearwater, Fla. He worked hard to clean up his life and took batting practice regularly. By the end of 2006, he had appeared in 15 games at low-level Class-A.

To Tampa's surprise, the Cincinnati Reds took a flyer on him in the Rule 5 Draft. In turn, Hamilton surprised the Reds by batting .403 in Spring Training, making the Opening Day roster and hitting .292 with 19 home runs and 47 RBI during the regular season. Still just 26 years old, he won the National League Comeback Player of the Year Award.

After the season ended, the Reds traded Hamilton to the Texas Rangers. There, the story of one of baseball's most unlikely resurrections would continue — including a record-setting performance at the 2008 Home Run Derby in Yankee Stadium.

ADRIAN GONZALEZ 2005

Before the 2000 First-Year Player Draft, Adrian Gonzalez drew comparisons to Mark Grace, Rafael Palmeiro and other first basemen who could hit for a high average and play Gold Glove–caliber defense.

With no consensus on the top overall pick, the cash-strapped Florida Marlins focused on drafting the best player they thought they could sign. So they selected Gonzalez, who hit .645 with 13 home runs and 34 RBI as a senior at Eastlake High School in Southern California.

The pick proved to be a shrewd one, but in 2003 the Marlins dealt Gonzalez to the Texas Rangers for closer Ugueth Urbina, who played a key role in the team's unlikely march to a World Series championship. Gonzalez, who had hit 17 home runs in the Minors in both 2001 and '02, managed just five in three Minor League stops in 2003.

He made his Big League debut with the Rangers in 2004, collecting 10 hits in 42 at-bats. In 2005, he saw more substantial playing time, but hit just .227 with six homers in 150 at-bats. Prior to the 2006 season, Gonzalez was dealt again, going to the San Diego Padres along with pitcher Chris Young and outfielder Terrmel Sledge. This time, the team that traded him would regret the move immediately.

Gonzalez, who was raised in the San Diego area wearing Tony Gwynn's No. 19, thrived upon returning home, hitting .304 with 24 home runs and 82 RBI.

"I was happy just to get out of there because that was a frustrating time for me," Gonzalez said. "The Padres gave me an opportunity to play, and I'm grateful for the confidence that they had in me."

HR	RBI	AVG	SLG
6	17	.227	.407

CHIPPER JONES 1995

The Atlanta Braves caught a break in 1990 when high school pitcher Todd Van Poppel made it clear that he wanted no part of the long-struggling franchise. Instead, the Braves spent the No. 1 pick in the First-Year Player Draft on Larry "Chipper" Jones, a power-hitting shortstop from Florida whom team officials saw as the next Cal Ripken Jr. By 1994, Jones was expected to compete for a regular role on the Braves, by then the three-time defending champions of the National League East.

Instead, Jones spent the entire strike-shortened '94 season rehabbing a knee he blew out in Spring Training. "At times, I felt like the forgotten man," he later said.

Jones worked so hard rehabilitating his leg that the Braves let popular third baseman Terry Pendleton go before the 1995 campaign. Jones, who had struggled defensively at shortstop in the Minor Leagues, committed 25 errors as a rookie third baseman.

He made up for it offensively, though, batting .265 with 23 homers and 86 RBI, leading all rookies in runs and RBI, and finishing second in home runs, hits and walks. With his Southern drawl, quirky nickname and socks worn high in deference to recently retired Braves reliever Steve Bedrosian, Jones quickly became the Braves' most popular player since Dale Murphy.

Jones lost the NL Rookie of the Year Award to Hideo Nomo of the Dodgers, whom some did not consider a true rookie because of his long tenure playing in Japan. Still, Jones may have enjoyed his rookie season more than Nomo, as he was a key contributor in the Braves' run to their first World Series championship since 1957.

NO. 1 PICKS TO BE NAMED MVP

PLAYER	DRAFTED	MVP YEAR(S)
Alex Rodriguez	1993	2003, '05, '07
Chipper Jones	**1990**	**1999**
Ken Griffey Jr.	1987	1997
Jeff Burroughs	1969	1974

HR	RBI	AVG	H
23	86	.265	139

At 6 feet 4 inches and a lanky 180 pounds with a textbook left-handed swing, Strawberry reminded scouts of another promising Southern California product: Ted Williams.

DARRYL STRAWBERRY 1983

Darryl Strawberry was a three-sport star at Crenshaw High School in Los Angeles, the same school that produced Big League outfielder Ellis Valentine and NBA standout Marques Johnson. At 6 feet 4 inches and a lanky 180 pounds with a textbook left-handed swing, Strawberry reminded scouts of another promising Southern California product: Ted Williams.

"Ted Williams is an awfully large order," said George Bamberger, who managed the Mets

HR	RBI	AVG	OBP
26	74	.257	.336

for part of Strawberry's rookie season in 1983. "But if someone asked me, 'Who coming up will be another Ted Williams?' Well, I'd have to say Darryl Strawberry. Fifteen years from now this kid will turn out to be one of the greatest ever to play the game."

The top overall pick in the 1980 draft, Strawberry made steady progress through the struggling Mets' farm system. Facing the Reds in his Major League debut on May 6, 1983, he whiffed three times against Mario Soto, who befuddled the rookie with a combination of heat and change-ups. A month later, Strawberry was hitting .161 and Mets officials were considering shipping him back to Triple-A Tidewater (Va.).

Instead, Strawberry got on track. During the first game of a June 28 doubleheader against the Cardinals in St. Louis, he homered twice and had five RBI in the Mets' 10-1 win. Over the last 54 games of the season, he hit .313 with 14 home runs and 34 RBI. Despite the slow start, he finished the year with a .257 average to go with his 26 homers and 74 RBI, and was voted the National League Rookie of the Year.

The Mets won just 68 games in 1983, their seventh straight losing season. But with Strawberry anchoring the lineup, they soon would embark on the greatest five-year stretch in franchise history.

chapter 13

SEAMLESS TRANSITION

Most rookies arrive in the Majors as a bundle of frayed nerves and spend their first weeks, like the new kids at school, just trying to find their place. Then there are those who seem like seasoned veterans from the first moment they step onto the field. Whether it's because of finely polished skills or maturity beyond their years, some rookies can't help but step into leadership roles at a young age. Some, such as Tom Seaver in 1967 and Fred Lynn in 1975, all but will their teams to another level. Then there's Jackie Robinson, who in 1947 endured a rookie season unlike any other, setting the standard for strength of character.

JACKIE ROBINSON 1947

Jackie Robinson's rookie season in 1947 was *the* most important freshman campaign in the history of baseball, breaking a color barrier that had hung over the sport for six decades. A four-sport star at UCLA, Robinson had experienced first-hand the consequences of the segregationist Jim Crow laws and the pervasive racism that plagued the United States. Court-martialed (and acquitted) while in the Army for refusing to sit in the back of a bus, Robinson's resolve was well known even before Branch Rickey of the Brooklyn Dodgers tapped him to be the first African-American ballplayer to cross the Majors' color barrier.

Robinson had excelled with the Kansas City Monarchs in the Negro Leagues and for the Montreal Royals, a Dodgers farm team, in 1946. Still, he faced doubters and critics, solely because of his race, when he made the parent club out of Spring

HR	RBI	AVG	H
12	48	.297	175

Training the next year. Some of his own Dodgers teammates even threatened to boycott the season, and Robinson endured taunts and abuse from opposing players and racist fans. Playing first base exclusively as a rookie, Robinson responded to hate mail and death threats with his play, batting .297 with 12 home runs and a league-leading 29 stolen bases. He earned the Major League Rookie of the Year Award, presented at the time to just one first-year player in the NL and AL combined.

Already 28 years old in his rookie season, Robinson exuded a calmness and confidence in the face of pressure that validated Rickey's choice. Although he batted .311 over a successful 10-year career and was named to six All-Star teams, it was Robinson's strength of character in his rookie season that made him a legendary figure in American sports and a key figure in his country's history.

SEAMLESS TRANSITION

GEORGE WRIGHT 1871

A shortstop with great range and a strong arm, George Wright was baseball's first "franchise player." Born in 1847, he played both professional cricket and amateur baseball during the Civil War before focusing full time on baseball with the Union Club of Morrisania in 1866.

When George's older brother, Harry, was hired in 1869 to manage baseball's first professional team, the Cincinnati Red Stockings, the first player he signed was George. The Wrights joined the Boston Red Stockings when the National Association was formed in 1871. George anchored the team at shortstop, where he became the first player to move away from the baseline when fielding. It was his practice of dropping pop flies to convert them into double plays that led to the infield fly rule.

Wright batted .413 in 1871 for the third-place Red Stockings, who would win the next four pennants.

RBI	AVG	OBP	SLG
11	.413	.453	.625

TROY TULOWITZKI 2007

Playing in his first Big League season in 2007, Troy Tulowitzki hit 24 home runs — a record for an NL rookie shortstop — turned the 13th unassisted triple play of all time, and led the Colorado Rockies to their first World Series appearance. At 6 foot 3, 205 pounds, the 22-year-old drew comparisons to Cal Ripken Jr. for his build and for his maturity and leadership.

"There are a lot of guys I can learn from in this locker room," he said. "But if I have something to say, I will say it."

HR	RBI	AVG	H
24	99	.291	177

Tulowitzki did his part, going 4 for 7 in a one-game tiebreaker with the Padres to clinch the NL Wild Card. He lost the NL Rookie of the Year Award to Brewers slugger Ryan Braun in one of the closest votes ever.

DEREK JETER 1996

A multi-talented athlete, Derek Jeter was selected sixth overall in the 1992 First-Year Player Draft. But his mental approach to the game soon became just as important as his physical assets.

Even as a 22-year-old rookie during the 1996 campaign, Jeter showed the type of leadership skills that would eventually earn him the role of team captain. He emerged as the first home-grown superstar the Yankees had developed since Don Mattingly, the club's previous captain.

Playing shortstop under the New York spotlight, on a team facing high expectations following a playoff appearance, Jeter appeared calm and poised. He impressed veterans with his work ethic, hard-nosed play and respect for the game.

"He's not intimidated by any situation," said catcher Joe Girardi, who would later manage in the Bronx, "and to be a leader, you have to be like that. He's well respected. He's able to make light of a lot of situations, to keep guys relaxed."

In 1996, Jeter batted .314 with 10 home runs and 78 RBI, and was a unanimous selection as the AL Rookie of the Year. In the postseason, he collected 22 hits and scored 12 runs while helping the Yankees to their first World Series title since 1978.

HR	RBI	AVG	H
10	78	.314	183

Lynn (scoring)

FRED LYNN 1975

A two-time All-American at the University of Southern California and the second-round pick of the Red Sox in 1973, Fred Lynn entered Spring Training in 1975 looking to compete with Jim Rice, Bernie Carbo and Tony Conigliaro for the left-field job.

Instead, Lynn's outfield range and quick left-handed bat prompted Manager Darrell Johnson to bump Juan Beniquez and Rick Miller in favor of Lynn in center field. With slugging catcher Carlton Fisk out for much of the year with a broken hand, Lynn often hit clean-up against right-handers.

"I never let the rookie part of it enter into my thinking, because if a kid knows he can hit, pressure isn't going to bother him," Johnson said. "And the reason I've used Fred in the No. 4 spot so often is because he gives me confidence."

Lynn got off to a hot start, batting .381 with 13 RBI in his first dozen games, including a two-homer performance at Yankee Stadium on April 16. On June 18 at Tiger

HR	RBI	AVG	SLG
21	105	.331	.566

Stadium, he hit three homers, a triple and an infield single against the Tigers, good for a rookie-record 16 total bases and 10 RBI.

Lynn established another rookie record by leading the AL with 47 doubles. He also became the first rookie to lead the AL in slugging percentage (.566). In addition to pacing the league in runs scored (103), Lynn was second in batting (.331), third in RBI (105) and fourth in total bases (299). He became the first rookie honored as both Rookie of the Year — had he not split a first-place vote with teammate Rice, he would have been a unanimous winner — *and* MVP. He also won the first of four Gold Glove Awards.

Lynn hit .364 in Boston's three-game sweep of the A's in the ALCS, provided two hits in Game 1 of the World Series against the Reds, and launched a three-run homer in Game 6 to cap one of the greatest rookie seasons ever.

ROOKIES TO LEAD THE LEAGUE IN SLUGGING PERCENTAGE		
PLAYER	SLG	YEAR
Fred Lynn	**.566**	**1975**
Mark McGwire	.618	1987
Ryan Braun	.634	2007

EVAN LONGORIA 2008

Evan Longoria did not have a typical rookie season in 2008. Just six days after arriving in the Majors, he signed a contract worth a guaranteed $17.5 million over six years and potentially $44 million over nine.

In July, he became the first rookie third baseman to be selected for the All-Star Game in 20 years. He competed in the Home Run Derby, and during the All-Star Game delivered a key RBI double, helping the AL to a 4-3 win. Just 22 years old, he impressed teammates and coaches in Tampa Bay with his maturity as much as with his powerful bat and Gold Glove–caliber defense.

"He's always in the moment and has this way about him where you know he's not going to be overwhelmed by any situation," Rays Manager Joe Maddon said. "And that speaks beyond his skill level. He's just very confident in a non-cocky way."

Although Longoria had a monster spring, he was sent down to Triple-A Durham to start the season before getting called up to the Bigs on April 12. Despite the delayed call-up and a stretch of 30 games that he missed with a wrist injury, he still hit 27 home runs, drove in 85 runs and won the AL Rookie of the Year Award. Longoria was a major part of how the Rays engineered one of the greatest turnarounds in baseball history, reaching the World Series just one year after finishing last in the AL East. In the postseason, Longoria hit six homers and drove in 13 runs.

"This kid is so humble even though he's already considered a superstar," said teammate Carlos Pena. "He's not afraid to laugh at himself and doesn't take himself too seriously. To have that level of maturity at any age, let alone 23, is very impressive."

HR	RBI	AVG	SLG
27	85	.272	.531

TOM SEAVER 1967

The New York Mets won just 66 games in 1966, the club's fifth season of expansion struggles. In 1967, they got a glimmer of hope in the form of pitcher Tom Seaver. Although he was just 22 years old, Seaver had been hardened by a stint in the U.S. Marine Corps Reserves and was not about to take losing lightly.

W	L	ERA	IP
16	13	2.76	251

"Some people who'd watched the Mets stumble through their first five seasons cracked jokes after the game," Seaver recalled. "'Break up the Mets. They've reached .500. From here on, it's all downhill.' I didn't laugh. I hadn't been raised on the Mets legend; I wasn't part of that losing history."

Seaver inspired his teammates, whose play improved with "Tom Terrific" on the mound. By the All-Star break, he was 8-5 with a 2.65 ERA and was chosen to represent the Mets in the Midsummer Classic. Seaver appeared so youthful that NL teammate Lou Brock mistook him for a batboy.

For the season, he went 16-13 with a 2.76 ERA, accounting for more than one-fourth of the Mets' wins. The NL Rookie of the Year tied for second in the league with 18 complete games, and helped lay the groundwork for what would become a remarkable Mets championship two years later.

GIL McDOUGALD 1951

Although not nearly as touted as Mickey Mantle, his fellow rookie on the New York Yankees, Gil McDougald enjoyed a more impressive freshman campaign in 1951 than his legendary Hall-of-Fame teammate.

Batting with an open stance, feet far apart, McDougald hit .306 with 14 home runs and 63 RBI. On May 3, the California native drove home six runs in one frame — tying a Big League record. Split-

HR	RBI	AVG	SB
14	63	.306	14

ting time between third base and second, he displayed the sparkling defense that would be his calling card throughout his 10-year career. He also scored 72 runs, posted an OBP of .396 and stole 14 bases, which would be a career high.

McDougald won the American League Rookie of the Year Award over Minnie Minoso in a close vote, even though Minoso had a more productive season statistically. In the 1951 Fall Classic, McDougald became the first rookie ever to hit a postseason grand slam, helping the New York Yankees to their first of five titles in his tenure.

JIM GILLIAM 1953

Jim Gilliam was nicknamed "Junior" while playing in the Negro Leagues for the Baltimore Elite Giants, where he was an All-Star from 1948 to 1950. Born in Nashville, Tenn., the young-looking Gilliam earned his moniker because he began playing semi-pro ball at age 14.

Signed by the Brooklyn Dodgers in 1951, Gilliam led the International League in runs in '51 and '52 while playing for the Montreal

HR	RBI	AVG	H
6	63	.278	168

Royals. The 24-year-old was so impressive that Dodgers Manager Chuck Dressen shifted his All-Star second baseman Jackie Robinson to the outfield and third base to make room at second for the heralded prospect in the spring of 1953.

The move paid off immediately, as Gilliam became the first NL rookie since 1899 to collect 100 walks. He scored 125 runs, just eight short of the post-1901 record established by Lloyd Waner in 1927. Gilliam also led the NL with 17 triples and 710 plate appearances, and won the NL Rookie of the Year Award over Harvey Haddix of the Cardinals.

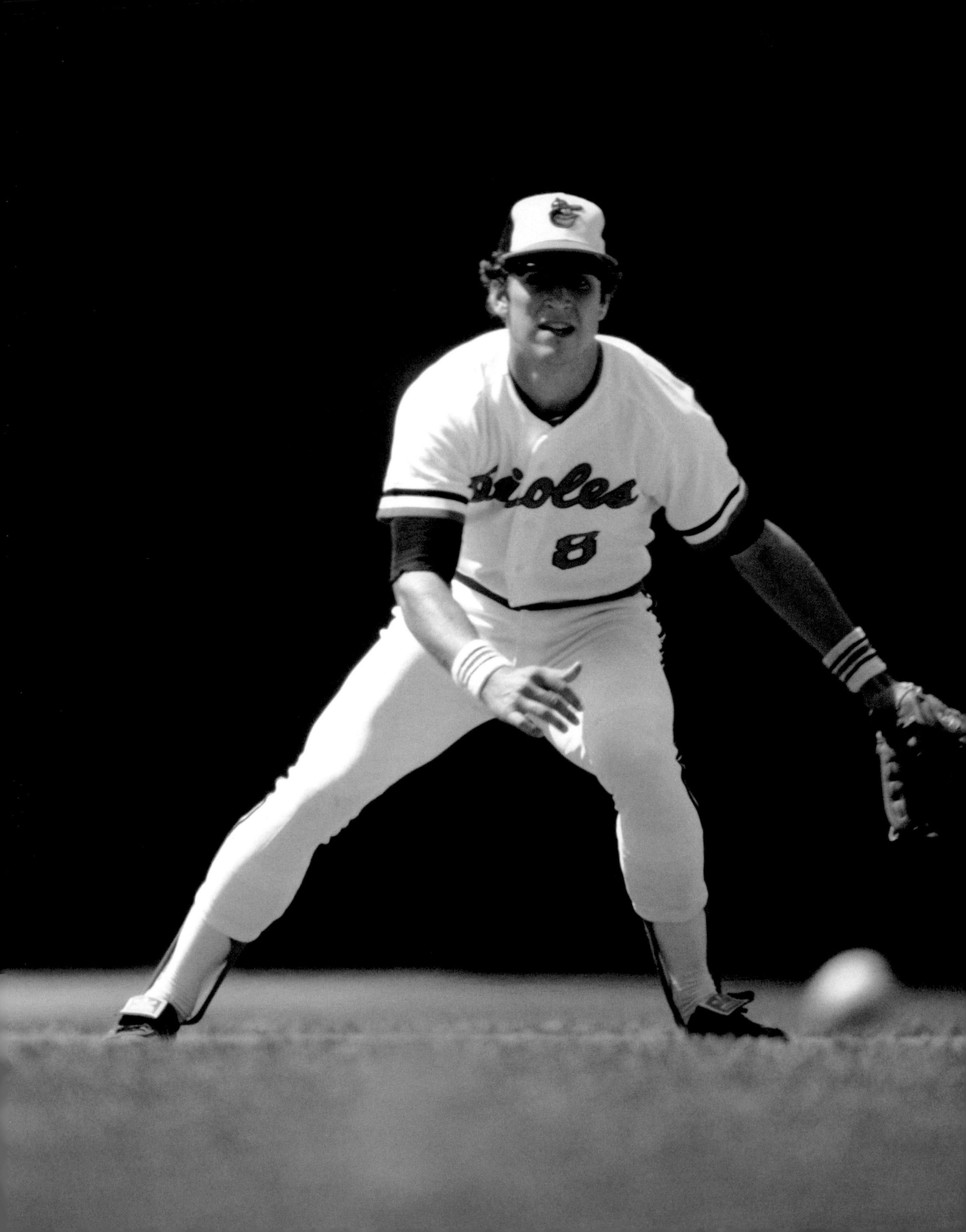
Orioles
8

CAL RIPKEN JR. 1982

Cal Ripken Jr. grew up in the world of baseball, following his father to various Minor League managerial outposts. By the time he made his Big League debut with the Baltimore Orioles on Aug. 10, 1981, he was a second-generation baseball lifer at the age of 20.

The Orioles envisioned the younger Ripken, their second-round pick in the 1978 draft, as their future third baseman. Even though Ripken batted just .128 in a 23-game stint in '81, the team traded veteran Doug DeCinces to the Angels before the 1982 season to free the position for their youngster.

On Opening Day against the Royals, Ripken homered and went 3 for 5 before going 4 for 55. Manager Earl Weaver kept the rookie in the lineup but sat him for the second game of a doubleheader on May 29, 1982. Ripken was back in the lineup the following day, and would not miss a game for the next 16 years — a streak of 2,632 contests.

HR	RBI	AVG	H
28	93	.264	158

On July 1, Ripken arrived at the ball-park to find his name penciled in at shortstop rather than third base because Weaver had struggled to find a successor to Mark Belanger, the perennial Gold Glover who had signed with the Dodgers during the offseason. Standing 6 feet 4 inches and weighing 225 pounds, Ripken was anything but the prototypical shortstop. But Ripken reminded Weaver of Marty Marion, who at 6 foot 2 had played the position admirably for the Cardinals in the 1940s and early '50s.

"When I took the field that day, I was under the impression that this stint at shortstop was only temporary," Ripken wrote years later. "But it lasted 15 years."

Ripken batted .264 for the season with 28 home runs and 93 RBI and won the Rookie of the Year Award, setting the stage for perhaps the most memorable season of his career.

chapter 14

LATE-SEASON CALL-UPS

Some rookies don't get a chance to begin their Big League careers at the start of a new season. Whether stuck behind an established player or sent back to the Minors for added experience, it can be frustrating to wait for the call to the Bigs. But there's perhaps nothing more exciting than a late-season call-up who pays immediate dividends, especially for a contender. From Joe Sewell in 1920 to Bob "Hurricane" Hazle in 1957 to more recent call-ups, such as Shane Spencer, Miguel Cabrera and Joba Chamberlain, baseball history is replete with young players who have changed the course of pennant races as late-season arrivals.

STAN MUSIAL 1941

Lost amid Joe DiMaggio's 56-game hitting streak, Ted Williams' .406 batting average and the rest of the magical 1941 season was the rise of a washed-out pitcher from the lower rungs of the Minor Leagues all the way to the Majors, where he debuted as an outfielder.

Stan Musial was a promising left-handed hurler until he fell on his shoulder while making a diving catch in the outfield in 1940, effectively ending his pitching career.

HR	RBI	AVG	SLG
1	7	.426	.574

The injury hastened what was probably an inevitable transition, although it was hardly as smooth as the swing Musial produced from his signature coiled stance.

Coming out of Spring Training in 1941, the Cardinals' Minor League managers were hardly fighting for the services of a player with an uncertain future. Ollie Vanek, manager of the Class-C team in Springfield, Mo., who had originally lobbied for Musial's signing, selected the pitcher-turned-outfielder for his squad.

Vanek, a former Minor League outfielder, tutored Musial on playing the position, and the 20-year-old learned quickly. Musial figured he would spend the year in Springfield, but after hitting .379 with 26 homers and 94 RBI, he was promoted to Double-A Rochester. There, he hit .326 in 54 games and helped the Red Wings to the playoffs; he got the call to St. Louis shortly thereafter.

His arrival came at the perfect time since the Cardinals had just lost Enos Slaughter to an injury and were in need of a left-handed bat in the outfield. Musial batted .426 in his 12-game stint, providing 20 hits for the Cardinals, who were battling Brooklyn for the National League pennant. The injury-plagued Redbirds won 97 contests but finished 2.5 games behind the Dodgers. The transition of Musial from dead-armed pitcher to promising outfielder was complete, and the Cardinals' record books would never be the same.

MUSIAL'S
BAT

LOUISVILLE SLUGGER
125
HILLERICH & BRADSBY CO.
MADE IN U.S.A.
LOUISVILLE KY.

Powerized

GENUINE

Stan Musial

LOUISVILLE SLUGGER

DUSTER MAILS 1920

A star of the Pacific Coast League who played briefly in the Big Leagues for Brooklyn in 1915 and '16, Walter Mails was purchased from the PCL by Cleveland late in the 1920 season. The left-handed Mails, nicknamed "Duster" for his hard fastball, provided the Indians with an immediate boost just as the Deadball Era ended and an age of slugging began.

Mails went 7-0 with a 1.85 ERA in nine appearances, eight of which were starts.
He delivered two shutouts, including a four-hitter against the Washington Senators on Sept. 16 that launched the Indians into first place to stay.

W	L	ERA	IP
7	0	1.85	63.1

Mails was even more impressive in the World Series against Brooklyn. In Game 3, he relieved Ray Caldwell with one out and a 2-0 deficit in the first inning, stranding both inherited runners and pitching six more innings of scoreless ball, albeit in a losing effort. Four days later, he pitched a three-hit shutout in Game 6, one day before Cleveland won its first ever World Series title.

JOE SEWELL 1920

When the Cleveland Indians' talented shortstop Ray Chapman died after being struck in the head by a pitch from the Yankees' Carl Mays on Aug. 16, 1920, the reeling Tribe quickly needed to find a replacement.

Harry Lunte temporarily manned the position before Cleveland summoned the 5-foot-7 Joe Sewell from the Minor Leagues. Once Sewell debuted on Sept. 10, the job remained his for most of the decade. In 22 games that first year, he batted .329, striking out just four times in 70 at-bats.

RBI	AVG	SLG	OBP
12	.329	.414	.413

The University of Alabama product batted just .174 in the Tribe's seven-game World Series victory over Brooklyn, but he had established himself as a rising star at just 21 years of age.

Playing his first full season in 1921, Sewell batted .318 with four home runs, 93 RBI and 101 runs, fanning just 17 times in 572 at-bats. He ranks as the toughest player in baseball history to strike out, whiffing just 114 times in 7,132 at-bats, a 1.6 percent rate.

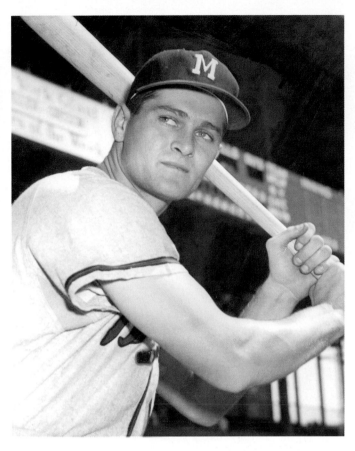

BOB 'HURRICANE' HAZLE 1957

Although Bob Hazle did not join the Milwaukee Braves until the 100th game of the 1957 season, he stormed onto the diamond, earning the nickname "Hurricane" after the meteorological Hurricane Hazel that battered his native South Carolina in 1954.

Hazle actually debuted with the Reds late in the 1955 season, appearing in six games. Traded to Milwaukee in April 1956, he was promoted from Wichita late in '57 when Braves outfielder Bill Bruton suffered a season-ending knee injury.

HR	RBI	AVG	SLG
7	27	.403	.649

In 14 games from Aug. 9 through Aug. 25, Hazle hit .565 with five home runs and 19 RBI. The stretch included a key three-game sweep of the Cardinals, which helped seal the National League for Milwaukee; during the series Hazle had seven hits and five RBI.

For the season, Hazle batted .403 in 134 at-bats with seven home runs and 27 RBI, and he received a vote for Rookie of the Year. After 1957, the Hurricane was downgraded to a tropical depression, as he played only one more season in the Majors.

JOBA CHAMBERLAIN 2007

Joba Chamberlain rocketed through professional baseball in 2007, stopping at all three levels of the Minors before joining the Yankees in time for a postseason run. With 100 mph heat and a back story right out of Hollywood, Chamberlain became a fan favorite. Not wanting to tax the prized 21-year-old arm, Yankees management created "The Joba Rules" to limit his appearances and innings.

As Yankees brass debated how to employ Chamberlain in the future, he thrived as a set-up man to Mariano Rivera in '07, allowing just

W	L	ERA	IP
2	0	0.38	24

one earned run over 24 innings and striking out 34. But the enduring image of the rookie's season came against the Indians in Game 2 of the Division Series in Cleveland. Chamberlain was unable to deal with a swarm of tiny bugs called midges, which stuck to his neck and flew around his face as he tried to pitch. Chamberlain surrendered the tying run in the eighth and the Indians went on to win in the 11th en route to the series win. But the infestation didn't take away from the dominance that he displayed in his first season.

MIGUEL CABRERA 2003

When he reported to Spring Training in 2003, Miguel Cabrera was just 19 years old and had never played a game above the Single-A level. After a brief stop with the Double-A Carolina Mudcats, Cabrera made his Major League debut on June 20 and smacked a game-winning homer in the 11th inning to give the Marlins a 3-1 victory. Cabrera was a well-known commodity; the Marlins thought so much of him that they paid a $1.8 million bonus to sign him out of Venezuela. But nobody expected him to come along so quickly.

Batting seventh and playing left field, Cabrera gave Marlins fans something to get excited about for the first time since the club's front office disbanded its 1997 world championship squad. When third baseman Mike Lowell broke his hand in September, Cabrera shifted to the hot corner, the position he had played in the Minor Leagues.

HR	RBI	AVG	SLG
12	62	.268	.468

Teammates marveled at his ferocious bat speed, comparing it to that of former Marlins slugger Gary Sheffield. "He's the real deal," said Jeff Conine, the only member of the 2003 Marlins to have played with Sheffield during his time in Florida as well. "He makes it look easy. The ball just does something extra when it comes off his bat."

"You get the feeling something good is going to happen every time he comes up to the plate," said Marlins Manager Jack McKeon.

While fellow rookie Dontrelle Willis anchored the rotation, Cabrera provided 12 home runs and 62 RBI in just 87 games. Facing the Cubs in the memorable 2003 National League Championship Series, Cabrera homered three times and drove in six runs. He added another home run in the Marlins' six game win over the Yankees in the World Series, capping a remarkable rookie season for a rising star.

Batting seventh and playing left field, Cabrera gave Marlins fans something to get excited about for the first time since the club's front office disbanded its 1997 world championship squad.

SHANE SPENCER 1998

During the last week of the 1998 season, late-season call-up Shane Spencer slammed six homers, had 15 RBI and won AL Player of the Week honors. It was part of a remarkable stretch of 67 at-bats that included 10 home runs, three of which were grand slams.

The outburst prompted Yankees Manager Joe Torre to compare the baby-faced outfielder to Joe Hardy, the out-of-nowhere star of the Broadway musical *Damn Yankees*. Teammates dubbed him "Roy Hobbs" after the hero of *The Natural* because of his epic home runs and because, at 26, he was older than most rookies.

Before 1998, Spencer was not considered much of a prospect. A 28th-round pick in the 1990 draft, he was a replacement player during the 1995 strike. He shuttled between New York and Triple-A Columbus throughout '98 before sticking in September.

On Sept. 24, facing Tampa Bay at Yankee Stadium, Spencer hit his second grand slam as the Yankees won their franchise-record 111th game, eclipsing the mark set by the 1927 squad. By then, Spencer had become a folk hero at Yankee Stadium, even replacing Derek Jeter as the favored heartthrob among teenage girls.

In Spencer's first playoff at-bat, against Rangers pitcher Rick Helling, he crushed a solo shot in Game 2 of the Division Series. The next game, he hit a series-clinching homer in Texas amid threatening weather that was reminiscent of the *The Natural's* climactic scene.

Like former Yankee phenoms Brian Doyle and Kevin Maas, Spencer's momentum didn't last. The next spring, he was sent back to Triple-A. He played parts of seven years in the Majors, five with the Yankees, but never became a regular.

"I don't want to be a one-time guy," Spencer told *Sports Illustrated* early in the 1999 season while back in the farm system. "So many guys have been in the Minors, had their chance, and were never heard of again. This can't be the end of me."

HR	RBI	AVG	SLG
10	27	.373	.910

Ellsbury

chapter 15

WORLD SERIES ROOKIES

Some rookies are unfazed by the pressure of the World Series. From Babe Adams and Whitey Ford to Andruw Jones and Dustin Pedroia, baseball history is replete with examples of rookies who acted as if the Fall Classic was waiting for their arrival. For these players, the World Series spotlight can serve as a coming-out party of sorts, like it did for Jones, who homered in his first two World Series at-bats as a 19-year-old outfielder for the Atlanta Braves — in Yankee Stadium no less. For fans and teammates, there's perhaps no more pleasant surprise than seeing a rookie thrive in the Fall Classic.

DUSTIN PEDROIA & JACOBY ELLSBURY 2007

Dustin Pedroia had just started his professional career and Jacoby Ellsbury was still in college when the Boston Red Sox won the World Series in 2004, so they never had to handle queries about curses, Bill Buckner, 1918 or 86-year droughts. As Sox rookies in 2007, their only firsthand experience came from playing for a well-balanced juggernaut expected to contend for a pennant and a world championship each year.

HR	RBI	AVG	H
1	7	.353	12

*Combined World Series Stats

"I got drafted the year they won the World Series, so I know that was a special time for them," Pedroia said during the '07 season. "As soon as I got up here, that was my mindset. I wanted to win a World Series like they did."

Pedroia, the pesky, pint-sized second baseman with the phenomenal work ethic, was hitting just .172 on May 1 of his rookie season. Fans wanted the Red Sox to start Alex Cora, a backup player who was hitting .360. Instead, Red Sox management's patience paid dividends as Pedroia rebounded to bat .317 for the season with eight homers and 50 RBI.

Ellsbury spent much of 2007 in the Minors, but emerged as a vital player late in the year, providing speed on the basepaths and range in the outfield. After Boston beat Colorado in Games 1 and 2 of the World Series, Manager Terry Francona moved Ellsbury to the leadoff spot, where he went 4 for 5 with two RBI in Game 3. Batting second, Pedroia went 3 for 5 as the Sox won, 10-5. Ellsbury added two more hits in Game 4 as Boston completed a Series sweep. Pedroia, generously listed at 5 foot 9, would be named AL Rookie of the Year two weeks later.

"Everyone doubted me at every level I've been at, saying I'm too small, not fast enough, my arm's not strong enough," Pedroia said. "There are people that have stuck by me and knew deep down that there's something about me that makes me a winning player."

WORLD SERIES ROOKIES

BABE ADAMS 1909

Babe Adams had an impressive rookie campaign in 1909, finishing 12-3 with a minuscule 1.11 ERA while pitching 130 innings over 12 starts and 13 relief appearances. After appearing in one game for the Cardinals in 1906 and four for the Pirates the following season, he finally settled in Pittsburgh, a late bloomer at age 27.

Even with his hard fastball and sharp curve, Adams was no guarantee to see time in the World Series. The Pirates won 110 games behind the pitching of Howie Camnitz (25-6), Vic Willis (22-11), Lefty Leifield (19-8) and Nick Maddox (13-8).

An hour and a half before Game 1 of the Fall Classic, Adams was sitting on the bench joking with fellow young teammates about how he would pitch the Tigers if given a chance.

"It was strictly fooling," he recalled years later. "For we all knew the team was full of stars and we were only kids."

Yet Pirates skipper Fred Clarke shocked everyone with the decision to start Adams in Game 1, either because of a tip that the Tigers had struggled against a similar pitcher or simply because the skipper was impressed with the rookie's composure.

Relying heavily on his curve, Adams allowed just one run on six hits in Pittsburgh's 4-1 win. He gave up four runs in Game 5, but struck out eight in a six-hit, 8-4 win that gave the Pirates a 3-games-to-2 Series lead. In Game 7, he again gave up just six hits in an 8-0 shutout. The three six-hit complete games rank as the best rookie pitching performance ever in a World Series. No rookie would start and win a Game 7 again until the Angels' John Lackey in 2002.

W	L	ERA	IP
3	0	1.33	27

*World Series Stats

Lackey

JOHN LACKEY 2002

John Lackey began 2002 in Triple-A. The 6-foot-6 righty ended the year as the winning pitcher in Game 7 of the World Series, capping an improbable run for the Angels.

In Game 4, played on his 24th birthday, Lackey allowed three runs in five innings and took a no-decision. Manager Mike Scioscia handed him the ball for Game 7, not only because Ramon Ortiz was hurt, but also because he believed in the rookie.

W	L	ERA	IP
1	0	4.38	12.1

*World Series Stats

"A big part of it is his makeup," pitching coach Bud Black said. "He's confident. You can't discount experience. But a lot of times, youthful aggressiveness pays off."

Lackey finished his first Big League regular season with a record of 9-4, and tied for fourth for American League Rookie of the Year.

Rodriguez

FRANCISCO RODRIGUEZ 2002

When outfielder Tim Salmon needed someone to warm him up before the Angels' game on Sept. 18, 2002, reliever Francisco Rodriguez volunteered. The 20-year-old had just arrived in the Big Leagues and began firing fastballs at the veteran Salmon.

"The ball was moving in and out. I could barely catch it, it had so much movement," Salmon said. "I finally told him, 'Hey, *I'm* loosening up here, not you.'"

W	L	ERA	IP
1	1	2.08	8.2

*World Series Stats

Rodriguez was just getting started. He allowed no runs in five regular-season games, got two relief victories in both the ALDS and the ALCS, and won Game 2 of the Fall Classic against the Giants. The skinny righty with the flaming fastball had 28 K's over 18.2 innings for the "Rally Monkey" Angels, who would win their first World Series.

PEPPER MARTIN 1931

Johnny Leonard Roosevelt "Pepper" Martin was no ordinary rookie. He had seen action briefly in the Major Leagues in 1928 and 1930, and was already 27 when the 1931 regular season began.

After spending seven seasons in the Minors, the pint-sized Martin was frustrated with his lack of playing time and made his displeasure known to Cardinals General Manager Branch Rickey.

As Martin recalled later: "One day I got a hold of Branch Rickey and I said, 'Look, Mr. Rickey. I'm a little tired chasin' up and down these Minor Leagues, and if you can't use me here, why don't you trade me so I can play every day?'"

Instead, Rickey traded Taylor Douthit to the Reds in June, and Martin became the Cardinals' regular center fielder. He made the most of his opportunity, finishing the season batting .300 with seven home runs and 75 RBI.

Martin saved his finest work for the World Series, where the Cardinals faced the Philadelphia Athletics in a rematch of the 1930 Fall Classic. In Game 1, Martin went 3 for 4 with a double off 31-game-winner Lefty Grove, but St. Louis lost the contest, 6-2. The following day, he went 2 for 3, stole two bases and scored the only two runs of the game, as the Cardinals evened the Fall Classic. In Game 3, Martin again went 2 for 3 with two runs scored as St. Louis beat Grove this time. He added two more hits and a stolen base in Game 4. Altogether, he batted .500 for the Series with 12 hits, including four doubles and a home run. He also drove in five runs, scored five times and stole five bases for the victorious Cardinals.

HR	RBI	AVG	SB
1	5	.500	5

*World Series Stats

147

WORLD SERIES ROOKIES

ANDRUW JONES 1996

Andruw Jones was playing in Class-A ball, a few weeks shy of his 19th birthday, when the 1996 season began. A five-tool talent from Willemstad, Curacao, a Caribbean island of 150,000 near Venezuela, Jones was the latest far-flung discovery by the Atlanta Braves' tireless scouting department.

A baby-faced outfielder, Jones drew his biggest raves for his ability to cover vast stretches of the outfield. He climbed the Minor League ladder quickly and made his Major League debut in mid-August. Jones went 1 for 5 with an RBI and run scored in his first Big League appearance, an 8-5 win over the Phillies.

With Jones earning regular time in the outfield, the Braves stretched their division lead to 12.5 games on Aug. 30. As Atlanta rolled to the NL East title with a nucleus of young stars, Jones flew under the radar even as the defending World Series champions advanced to the Fall Classic for the fourth time in six seasons.

Facing the Yankees, who were in the World Series for the first time in 15 years, Jones introduced himself to a national audience by crushing two home runs in the Braves' Game 1 win in the Bronx. On the day that would have been Mickey Mantle's 65th birthday, he eclipsed "The Mick" as the youngest player to homer in the World Series, and joined Oakland's Gene Tenace (1972) as the only players to homer in their first two at-bats in a World Series.

"He makes it look easy," said teammate Chipper Jones. "Even at 19, he looks like he should be here."

"He's just a great, great player," added Braves Manager Bobby Cox. "He's not your normal 19-year-old."

HR	RBI	AVG	SLG
2	6	.400	.750

*World Series Stats

148

MULTIPLE HOME RUNS BY A ROOKIE IN THE WORLD SERIES			
PLAYER	TEAM	HR	YEAR
Charlie Keller	New York Yankees	3	1939
Jim Gilliam	Brooklyn Dodgers	2	1953
Tony Kubek	New York Yankees	2	1957
Chuck Essegian	Los Angeles Dodgers	2	1959
Reggie Smith	Boston Red Sox	2	1967
Willie McGee	St. Louis Cardinals	2	1982
Andruw Jones	**Atlanta Braves**	**2**	**1996**

LIVAN HERNANDEZ 1997

Before the 1997 season, Marlins Owner Wayne Huizenga committed $89 million to free agents in the hopes of winning a World Series and landing a new stadium for his club. Although the high-priced veterans played well, he may have gotten a far better return on his investment from a pair of low-priced 22-year-olds who barely spoke English at the time. Cuban pitcher Livan Hernandez and Colombian shortstop Edgar Renteria were as much a part of the Wild Card–winning Marlins' run to a World Series victory as veterans Kevin Brown, Bobby Bonilla and Gary Sheffield.

Hernandez, a Cuban defector in 1995, went 9-3 during the season, but was not added to the postseason rotation until Alex Fernandez got hurt during the NLDS. Struggling with culture shock and adjusting to life without his half-brother, Orlando — a future Yankees hero who was still in Cuba at the time — he took refuge on the mound, twice beating the Braves in the NLCS to win MVP honors.

W	L	ERA	IP
2	0	5.27	13.2

*World Series Stats

"He's been through a lot and that's enabled him to handle these situations better," said Marlins pitching coach Larry Rothschild.

Like Hernandez, Renteria — in his second Big League season — kept mostly to himself in 1997, especially after Opening Day second baseman Luis Castillo was sent to the Minors. But the skinny, slick-fielding shortstop had a knack for clutch, late-inning hits, including a game-winning single in the Division Series against the Giants.

With growing awareness of Hernandez's quest to bring his mother and half-brother to America, the right-hander won Games 1 and 5 of the World Series, becoming the toast of South Florida. Cleveland won Game 6 in Miami and was two outs from winning the Series when the Marlins sent the game into extra innings. Florida loaded the bases in the 11th before Renteria provided another game-winning hit — this time a World Series–clinching hit — sending Miami into a fevered, bilingual frenzy.

ALFONSO SORIANO 2001

Coming off four world titles in five years, the Yankees expected greatness from Alfonso Soriano in 2001. With Derek Jeter at shortstop and depth in the outfield, "Sori" found a spot when Chuck Knoblauch got the throwing yips at second.

Soriano lived up to expectations, batting .268 with 18 homers, 73 RBI and 43 steals. Still, the 25-year-old had rookie moments.

HR	RBI	AVG	H
1	2	.240	6

*World Series Stats

He committed 19 errors at his new position and drew negative attention in the playoffs for not running out what he mistakenly thought was a home run, and then on defense for getting to second late and not completing a double play.

But he did provide a walk-off home run against the Mariners in Game 4 of the ALCS, and hit what would have been the World

'BULLET' JOE BUSH 1913

Leslie Ambrose Bush is best known as a pioneer of the forkball, for helping Babe Ruth find his way home from the bar during their six years as teammates with the Red Sox and Yankees, and for a memorable rookie performance during the 1913 World Series.

During Bush's one season in the Minors before his ascension to the Majors, the club president in Missoula, Mont., called him Joe Bush after an eclectic man who hung around the team office. The righty became "Bullet" Joe after launching a rock at a hen out in the fields, killing the fowl. "It was a one in a million shot," he said.

W	L	ERA	IP
1	0	1.00	9

*World Series Stats

Pitching for a powerhouse A's team as a rookie in 1913, he went 15-6 with a 3.82 ERA and six complete games. Although just 20 years old in his first season, he started Game 3 of the World Series and beat the Giants, 8-2, in front of 36,896 at the Polo Grounds, at the time a record attendance for a Fall Classic game. He allowed just five hits and one earned run, going the distance for the A's, who would win the Series in five games.

Bush went on to play 17 seasons in the Majors, winning 195 games and World Series titles with the Athletics, 1918 Red Sox and 1923 Yankees. In his fourth season, Bush won 15 games for a Philadelphia Athletics team that won just 36 all season.

Series–winning homer in Game 7 if not for a blown save by Mariano Rivera. In Game 5 of the Series, Soriano delivered a single in the bottom of the 12th to give the Yankees an extra-inning walk-off for the second time in two nights.

"I never thought that would ever happen again," Soriano said. "It felt like an out-of-body experience, like we're here but we're not here."

Ford (center)

WHITEY FORD 1950

In the spring of 1950, the Yankees invited Edward "Whitey" Ford, 21, to Spring Training. There he joined the likes of Joe DiMaggio and Yogi Berra under the watchful eye of Manager Casey Stengel.

Both the young lefty and Stengel realized he needed more seasoning, so Ford began the year with the club's top farm team. By July, the Yankees needed pitching help and called up Ford, who grew up a few miles from Yankee Stadium in the Astoria neighborhood of Queens. Between Stengel's nurturing and his own quick development, Ford went 9-1 with a 2.81 ERA and seven complete games, playing a key role in the Yankees' run to the pennant. Ford's win over Detroit on Sept. 16 propelled the Yankees into first place for good.

For all of Ford's immediate success, he was the fourth starter and there was question as to whether he would pitch in the World Series, where the Yankees faced the Phillies. After New York won the first three games, Stengel felt comfortable giving the ball to the rookie in Game 4. Ford pitched a gem and would win the clinching game, but when the Phillies mounted a rally with two outs in the ninth, Stengel replaced him.

"I was ticked when Casey came to get me," Ford said. "I didn't want to come out, but what was really strange was when I was walking to the dugout, everyone was booing! I couldn't figure out why they were booing after I'd pitched this game. Then I turned around and saw Casey walking right behind me and I realized they were booing him!

"I'd gotten tickets for about 30 of my friends and relatives and they were booing as well. Casey was no dummy. He wasn't about to walk back to the dugout by himself."

FORD'S CAREER WORLD SERIES STATS

W	L	CG	ERA	IP	K
10	8	7	2.71	146	94

W	L	ERA	IP
1	0	0.00	8.2

*World Series Stats

SOURCE NOTES

CHAPTER 1

9. "Pujols on La Russa, promotion" Verducci, Tom. "Wild Card." *Sports Illustrated* 1 Oct. 2001.

9. "Pujols on Rookie of the Year" Published at USA Today.com on Nov. 12, 2001; retrieved June 1, 2009.

10. "Scoop Latimer on Jackson" Historic Baseball. "Jackson Story Still Captivating to Fans. Published at historicbaseball.com; retrieved June 1, 2009.

10. "Jackson on batting title" Johnson, Lloyd & Brenda Ward. *Who's Who in Baseball History*. 1994. Brompton Books, pg. 213.

12. "Like a right-handed Don Mattingly" Hohlfeld, Neil. "Bagwell Selected Top N.L. Rookie." *The Houston Chronicle* 7 Nov. 1991.

12. "I remember Jeff Bagwell" Hohlfeld, Neil. "Bagwell Selected Top N.L. Rookie." *The Houston Chronicle* 7 Nov. 1991.

12. "I started looking at everything" Hohlfeld, Neil. "Bagwell Selected Top N.L. Rookie." *The Houston Chronicle* 7 Nov. 1991.

13. "Mauch: Allen a sure bet" King, Kelley. "Dick Allen, Baseball Bad Boy." *Sports Illustrated* 19 July 1999.

13. "Philly wasn't ready" Lidz, Franz "Whatever Happened to Dick Allen?" *Sports Illustrated* 19 July 1993.

13. "Pinson had yet to learn how to get a good jump" Terrell, Roy. "Baseball Is A Breeze For Vada Pinson " *Sports Illustrated* 31 August 1959.

13. "Vada is making a joke out of this game" Terrell, Roy. "Baseball Is A Breeze For Vada Pinson." *Sports Illustrated* 31 August 1959.

14. "One of Oliva's friends" Published at tonyoliva.com; retrieved June 2, 2009.

14. "I'd see him around the cage" Deford, Frank. "Home Run Heaven." *Sports Illustrated* 18 May 1964.

15. "He made his professional baseball debut" Von Borries, Philip. "Pete Browning: The Original Louisville Slugger," Published at jockbio.com; retrieved June 2, 2009.

15. "Already battling alcohol" Von Borries, Philip. "Pete Browning" The SABR Baseball Biography Project. Published at bioproj.sabr.org; retrieved June 2, 2009.

16. "Jobe on Martinez' stature" Newhan, Ross. "This deal was a heartbreaker for Dodgers." *The Los Angeles Times* 22 April 2008.

16. "It's still my motivation" Newhan, Ross. "This deal was a heartbreaker for Dodgers." *The Los Angeles Times* 22 April 2008.

17. "Mike hits it harder than I did" Whiteside, Kelly. "A Piazza with Everything." *Sports Illustrated* 5 July 1993.

18. "McHale: Like trading Lou Brock" Kaplan, Jim. "Raines Really Pours it On." *Sports Illustrated* 11 May 1981.

19. "A gangly shortstop when drafted in 1994" Williams, Pete. "An All-Star's Big Build Up." *USA Today Baseball Weekly* 1 March 2000.

19. "Selc: I don't know anyone more driven" Verducci, Tom. "A Cut Above." *Sports Illustrated* 5 March 2001.

19. "Nomar under a microscope" Crothers, Tim. "Garciaparra's Strong Start." *Sports Illustrated* 19 May 1997.

CHAPTER 2

20. "Sports writer Terry Pluto of the Plain Dealer dubbed him Super Joe" Wulf, Steve. "Super Joe: A Legend in His Own Time." *Sports Illustrated* 8 September 1980.

20. "I really wasn't a franchise player" Lidz, Franz. "Flashes in the Pan." *Sports Illustrated* 4 May 1992.

22. "Considered an unusually fast worker" Enders, Eric. The SABR Baseball Biography Project: George McQuillan. Published at bioproj.sabr.org; retrieved June 3, 2009.

22. "Jimmy Callahan marveled" Smiley, Richard. The SABR Baseball Biography Project: Reb Russell. Published at bioproj.sabr.org; retrieved June 4, 2009.

23. "I was 18 all over again" Goldstein, Richard. "Joe Black, Pitching Pioneer for the Dodgers, Dies at 78." *The New York Times* 18 May 2002.

23. "Dressen encouraged Black to add more pitches" The Associated Press 17 May 2002 Published at USAToday.com; retrieved June 3, 2009.

25. "There's a fine line" Fimrite, Ron. "For All You Do, this Hug's For You." *Sports Illustrated* 1 November 1982.

26. "You'd never throw him out" Goldstein, Richard. "Sam Jethroe is Dead at 83; Was Oldest Rookie of the Year." *The New York Times* 19 June 2001.

26. "Every ball he threw" "Indians Pitcher Gene Bearden Dies at 83." *The Palm Beach Post*. 19 March 2004.

27. "He told the Cleveland Plain Dealer" McDonald, Brian. *Indian Summer: The Tragic Story of Louis Francis Sockalexis, the First Native American in Major League Baseball*. Rodale Books, 2003. p.78-79.

28. "I think he threw 100 miles an hour" Dolgan, Bob. "Former Indians Broadcaster Herb Score At Age 75." *The Cleveland Plain Dealer* 11 November 2008.

28. "We wouldn't sell him for $2 million" Dolgan, Bob. "Former Indians Broadcaster Herb Score At Age 75." *The Cleveland Plain Dealer* 11 November 2008.

28. "The greatest left-handed pitcher who ever lived" Goldstein, Richard. "Herb Score, 75, Indians Pitcher Derailed by Line Drive, Dies." *The New York Times* 11 November 2008.

CHAPTER 3

30. "It felt like the end of me" Stump, Al. *Cobb: A Biography*. Algonquin Books, 1996. p. 22.

33. "Any kid of 19 has all these teenage habits" Deford, Frank. "Not Much To Do But Eat, Sleep and Play Baseball." *Sports Illustrated* 3 August 1964.

33. "Cedeno hadn't played as many as 100 games" Peterson, Harold. "Hail, Cesar! And Hello." *Sports Illustrated* 7 August 1972.

34. "Hernandez on Gooden being just 19" Hecht, Henry. "Goodeness Gracious!" *Sports Illustrated* 21 May 1984.

36. "Something went past me that made me flinch" Cobb, Ty with Al Stump. *My Life in Baseball: The True Record*. Garden City, NY; Doubleday and Company, 1961.

36. "The Sporting News had first mentioned the young slugger" Daniel, W. Harrison. *Jimmie Foxx: The Life and Times of a Baseball Hall of Famer: 1907–1967*. McFarland & Co, 2004.

37. "Del Crandall turned to Jim Wilson" Jordan, Pat. "Years Ahead of His Time." *Sports Illustrated* 29 July 1974.

38. "The press called him "Master Feller" Deford, Frank. "Rapid Robert Can Still Bring It." *Sports Illustrated* 8 August 2005.

CHAPTER 4

41. "We didn't bring him up because he's a good story" Romano, John. "Morris finally comes of age." *The St. Petersburg Times* 19 Sept. 1999: Page 1C.

42. "The trick is not to let them get on" Lueck, Thomas J. "Hoyt Wilhelm, First Reliever in the Hall of Fame, Dies." *The New York Times* 25 August 2002.

42. "We didn't have a great deal of time" Skipper, John C. *Dazzy Vance: A Biography of the Brooklyn Dodger Hall of Famer*. McFarland, 2007: p.17.

42. "Pitching with a motion so extreme" Okrent, Daniel. "Dazzling Dazzy." *Sports Illustrated* 21 June 1999.

45. "Class was the way to describe the guy" UPI. "Ex-Yank Great Elston Howard Dies at 51." *The Bulletin Journal of Cape Girardeau, Mo.* 16 December 1980: p.11.

46. "McGinnity was a magician in the box" Mack, Connie. *My 66 Years in the Big Leagues*. Dover Publications, 2009.

CHAPTER 5

48. "Much bigger than Valenzuela's situation" Williams, Pete. "The Real Thing." *USA Today Baseball Weekly* 31 May 1995: p.16.

48. "It takes a few pitches to figure him out" Williams, Pete. "The Real Thing." *USA Today Baseball Weekly* 31 May 1995: p.16.

50. "Sasaki was nicknamed 'Daimajin'" Whiting, Robert. "Lost in Translation." *Sports Illustrated* 22 March 2004.

50. "Happier than I ever was in Japan" Cannella, Stephen. "The Hot Corner (Seattle Mariners)." *Sports Illustrated* 16 October 2000.

51. "Lived alone in a Manhattan high rise" Whiting, Robert. "Lost in Translation." *Sports Illustrated* 22 March 2004.

53. "I don't think you can pitch him one way" Pearlman, Jeff. "Big Hit." *Sports Illustrated* 28 May 2001.

54. "He swings his hands over his head" Verducci, Tom. "The Riddle." *Sports Illustrated* 26 March 2007.

CHAPTER 6

57. "Attendance rose 400,000 from '75" Caple, Jim. "Fidrych was a wonderful one-of-a-kind phenomenon." Published at ESPN.com on 15 April 2009; retrieved June 10, 2009.

58. "Refreshing to see a guy so in awe of the big leagues" Ballard, Chris. "The Kid with the Kick." *Sports Illustrated* 30 June 2003.

61. "He's a big kid, a baby" Swift, E.M. "Bringing Up Junior." *Sports Illustrated* 7 May 1990.

63. "Sutton on Valenzuela's screwball" Kaplan, Jim. "Epidemic of Fernando Fever." *Sports Illustrated* 4 May 1981.

64. "Veeck placed a cigarette on the ground" Published at satchelpaige.com; retrieved June 10, 2009.

64. "You should'a seen me five or six years ago" Paige, LeRoy and David Lipman. *Maybe I'll Pitch Forever*. Bison Books, 1993, p.11.

CHAPTER 7

67. "Maas on 'the next Babe Ruth'" Rushin, Steve. "Attack of the Tater Tots" *Sports Illustrated* 24 September 1990.

67. "I was hot at the right time" McCarron, Anthony. "Where are they now? Former Yankee Kevin Maas is a solid investment." *New York Daily News* 4 October 2008.

69. "Crandall on Davis, Aaron, Mays" Maisel, Ivan. "At Last, A Man To Shout About." *Sports Illustrated* 11 June 1984.

73. "McGwire on being just a basic athlete" Fimrite, Ron. "The Bay Area Bombers." *Sports Illustrated* 4 April 1988.

73. "McGwire on never hitting 49 homers again" Fimrite, Ron. "The Bay Area Bombers." *Sports Illustrated* 4 April 1988.

74. "Melvin on Braun's expectations" McCalvy, Adam. "Braun Named Rookie of the Year." Published at MLB.com on 12 November 2007; retrieved June 11, 2009.

CHAPTER 8

76. "Wood on being focused" Wertheim, L. Jon. "Flame Thrower" *Sports Illustrated* 18 May 1998.

78. "Mauch on two great months from Rogers" Jordan, Pat. "Mr. Intensity of the Expos." *Sports Illustrated* 29 April 1974.

78. "Monbouquette on Radatz durability" Edes, Gordon. "Former Red Sox closer Radatz dies after fall." *The Boston Globe* 17 March 2005.

79. "Jackson on hoping for a Welch mistake" Fimrite, Ron. "No Place Like Home." *Sports Illustrated* 23 October 1978.

81. "Oswalt on his curveball" Pearlman, Jeff. "The Right Stuff." *Sports Illustrated* 8 July 2002.

CHAPTER 9

83. "Winfield on going to the Minors" Ludtke, Melissa. "Nobody Knows The Doubles I've Creamed." *Sports Illustrated* 11 July 1977.

84. "Doby on homering off Sain" The Associated Press. "Larry Doby, Breaker of a Color Barrier In Robinson's Wake, Is Dead at Age 79. *The New York Times*. 19 June 2003.

86. "Turner on Horner going straight to Majors" Papanek, John. "It's Horner at the Hot Corner." *Sports Illustrated* 14 April 1978.

86. "Horner on not wanting to go to Minors" Papanek, John. "It's Horner at the Hot Corner." *Sports Illustrated* 14 April 1978.

91. "Kaline was shy" Shapleu, Robert. "On the Lookout for a Kaline" *Sports Illustrated* 14 May 1956.

93. "Abbott blessed with pretty-good left arm" Hersch, Hank. "The Great Abbott Switch." *Sports Illustrated* 25 May 1987.

CHAPTER 10

95. "Robinson on signing for $3,500" Altobelli, Lisa. "They Said it Frank Robinson. *Sports Illustrated* 24 January 2005.

96. "Rigney comparing Cepeda to Mays" Creamer, Robert. "Giants: A Smash Hit in San Francisco." *Sports Illustrated* 16 June 1958.

101. "Murray on dealing with attention" Singer, Tom. "Murray lets down the wall at Hall." Published at MLB.com on July 27, 2003; retrieved June 17, 2009.

102. "Williams on happy first season. Boston, Talmage. *1939: Baseball's Tipping Point.* Bright Sky Press, 2005. p. 26.

CHAPTER 11

104. "Sisler a baseball freak" Thomas, Henry W. *Walter Johnson: Baseball's Big Train.* Washington, D.C.: Phenom Press, 1996: p.140.

104. "Sisler on beating Johnson" Carmichael, John F. *My Greatest Day in Baseball.* New York: A.S. Barnes and Company, 1945: p.157.

109. "DiMaggio was sparkling all afternoon" Childs, Kingsley. "Dickey's Two Homers Defeat Tigers, 6-5; DiMaggio Cuts Off Run; Throw on Fly Catches Fox, Who Strives for Tying Tally in 9th." *The New York Times* 8 May 1936: p.27.

110. "Lau calls Hurdle best Royals hitting prospect eve." Keith, Larry. "The Eternal Hopefuls of Spring." *Sports Illustrated* 20 March 1978.

110. "Schuerholz on Hurdle's potential" Keith, Larry. "The Eternal Hopefuls of Spring." *Sports Illustrated* 20 March 1978.

110. "Towers on Strasburg" Jenkins, Lee. "Stephen Strasburg is ready to bring it. *Sports Illustrated* 30 March 2009.

113. "Mays wanted to quit" Feeney, Charley. "Willie Mays Recalls His Rookie Year." *Baseball Digest* December 1973: p.40-41.

114. "The best high school pitcher I've ever seen" Passan, Jeff. "The arm that changed the Major League draft." Published at Yahoo! Sports on 5 June 2006; retrieved June 18, 2009.

115. "Mantle was scared more than anything else" Williams, Pete. "Mantle lives life of a true champion. *USA Today Baseball Weekly* 18 October 1991. p. 8-9.

115. "Mantle was promised $7,500" Richman, Milton. "Mantle Looks Back to His Rookie Year." *Baseball Digest* June 1981: p.52-54.

CHAPTER 12

117. "Rodriguez on Ripken" Williams, Pete. "Alex the Great." *USA Today Baseball Weekly* 28 August 1996: p. 28-30.

118. "LaMar on Hamilton" Topkin, Marc. "The Natural Choice." *The St. Petersburg Times* 3 June 1999.

120. "Gonzalez happy to get out of Texas" Verducci, Tom. "3 San Diego Padres." *Sports Illustrated* 26 March 2007.

121. "Jones felt like a forgotten man" Williams, Pete. "Jones contributes in un-rookie-like fashion." *USA Today Baseball Weekly* 11 October 1995: p.22.

122. "Bamberger on Williams, Strawberry" Nack, William. "The Perils of Darryl." *Sports Illustrated* 23 April 1984.

CHAPTER 13

126. "Tulowitzki on learning" McCallum, Jack. "Rocktoberfest." *Sports Illustrated* 15 October 2007.

127. "Mattingly told Jeter to run in" Olney, Buster. "Pinstriped for Greatness." *The New York Times* 21 March 1999.

127. "Girardi on Jeter" Olney, Buster. "Pinstriped for Greatness." *The New York Times* 21 March 1999.

129. "Johnson on using Lynn cleanup" Elderkin, Phil. "Fred Lynn: Best Rookie Hitter in A.L." *Baseball Digest* September. 1975: p. 20-22.

130. "Maddon on Longoria" Williams, Pete. "Year One." *MLB Insiders Club Magazine.* Vol. 2, Issue 1: p.57-59.

130. "Pena on Longoria" Williams, Pete. "Year One." *MLB Insiders Club Magazine.* Vol. 2, Issue 1: p.57-59.

132. "Seaver on Mets struggles" Golenbock, Peter. *Amazin': The Miraculous History of New York's Most Beloved Team.* St. Martin's Griffin, 2003, p.190.

135. "Ripken on moving to shortstop" Ripken, Cal with Donald T. Phillips. *Get in the Game.* Gotham Books, 2007: p.83.

CHAPTER 14

136. "Vanek tutored Musial" Stanton, Joseph. *Stan Musial: A Biography.* Greenwood, 2007: p.19

139. "Stormed onto the scene" Lidz, Franz. "Flashes in the Pan." *Sports Illustrated* 4 May 1992.

141. "Conine on Cabrera" Schmuck, Peter. "A Star in the Making." *Baseball Digest* August 2004.

141. "McKeon on Cabrera" Schmuck, Peter. "A Star in the Making." *Baseball Digest* August 2004.

143. "Torre compared Spencer to Joe Hardy" McCarron, Anthony. "Spencer: Shane-Sational. The New York *Daily News* 1 October 1998.

143. "Right out of The Natural" Olney, Buster. "Against Rangers, only Rain Stops the Yankees." *The New York Times* 3 October 1998.

143. "I don't want to be a one-time guy" Pearlman, Jeff. "Come Back Shane." *Sports Illustrated* 10 May 1999.

CHAPTER 15

145. "Pedroia on wanting to win a World Series" Curry, Jack. "Rookies Don't Have to Wait for a Title." *The New York Times* 28 October 2007.

145. "Pedroia on overcoming obstacles" The Associated Press. "Pedroia wins in landslide." 13 November 2007.

146. "Adams on 1909 World Series" Carmichael, John P. *My Greatest Day in Baseball.* New York: Barnes: 1945. p.199.

146. "Black on Lackey" The Associated Press "Kid Rocks: Lackey becomes first rookie since 1909 to win Game 7." 27 October 2002.

147. "Salmon on Rodriguez" Nightengale, Bob. "Bullpen out of sight, not out of mind." *USA Today Baseball Weekly* 16 October 2002.

147. "Martin approached Rickey" Carmichael, John P. *My Greatest Day in Baseball.* New York: Barnes: 1945: p.153.

148. "Jones makes it look easy" Curry, Jack. "Braves Rookie Leads Assault that Buries Yanks in Opener." *The New York Times* 21 October 1996.

148. "Jones just a great player" Curry, Jack. "Braves Rookie Leads Assault that Buries Yanks in Opener." *The New York Times* 21 October 1996.

151. "Rothschild on Hernandez" Williams, Pete. "Lonely Livan." *USA Today Baseball Weekly* 22 October 1997: p.18.

151. "Renteria kept mostly to himself" Williams, Pete. "Hernandez loses cool, heats up, hangs on." *USA Today Baseball Weekly* 29 October 1997: p.14.

151. "Conine on Renteria" Williams, Pete. "Dramatic 11th crowns Leyland, Fish kings." *USA Today Baseball Weekly* 29 October 1997: p. 16.

152. "Soriano had his rookie moments" White, Paul. "Diamondbacks Turn to Go After Yanks" *USA Today Baseball Weekly* 23 October 2001.

153. "Soriano: Like an outer body experience" Cannella, Stephen. "Welcome to the Club: Soriano joins Yankees' long list of clutch performers." Published at SI.com on 2 November 2001; retrieved June 25, 2009.

153. "A one in a million shot" Gallagher, Jack. "Bullet Joe Bush Remembers the Babe" *Baseball Digest* September 1972: p.66-68.

155. "Ford ticked when Stengel came to get him" Madden, Bill. "Whitey Ford's near shutout against Phillies is still World Series favorite." The New York *Daily News* September 17, 2008.

CREDITS

INDEX

Aaron, Hank, 37, 45, 69, 113
Abbott, Jim, 92-93
"Abbott Switch," 93
Abner, Shawn, 117
Adams, Babe, 54, 145-146
A Clever Baseballist, 96
Agee, Tommie, 101
Alexander, Dale, 68, 72, 109
Alexander, Grover Cleveland, 95, 100
Allen, Dick, 13, 28, 101
All-Star Game, 6, 9, 14, 16, 51, 53, 57, 63, 109, 130, 132
  1936, 109
  1951, 63
  1961, 6
  1964, 14
  1967, 132
  1976, 57
  1981, 63
  1999, 16
  2001, 9, 53
  2003, 51
  2009, 130
Alomar, Sandy Jr., 67
Alou, Felipe, 96
American Association, 15, 69
American League Championship Series (ALCS), 117, 129, 147, 152
  1975, 129
  1995, 117
  2001, 152
  2002, 147
Anaheim Angels, 146
Anderson, Dave, 84
Anderson, Matt, 104
Anson, Cap, 80
Appalachian League, 33
Arizona Diamondbacks, 54
Arizona State University, 86
Atlanta Braves, 25, 48, 83, 86, 106, 117, 121, 145, 148, 151
Atlanta Hawks, 83

Bagwell, Jeff, 9, 12
Baker Bowl, 42
Balboni, Steve, 67
Baltimore Elite Giants, 23, 133
Baltimore Orioles, 28, 46, 57, 101, 111, 135
Bamberger, George, 122
Banks, Ernie, 45
Barfield, Jesse, 67
Baseball America, 106, 114
Baseball Writers Association of America, 28
Baylor, Don, 28
Baylor University, 89
Bearden, Gene, 26, 55
Beazley, John, 55
Beckett, Josh, 118
Bedrosian, Steve, 121
Belanger, Mark, 135
Belcher, Tim, 55
Benes, Andy, 117
Beniquez, Juna, 129
Benson, Kris, 117
Berger, Wally, 72-74, 95
Berra, Yogi, 45, 91, 155
Berroa, Angel, 51
Biggio, Craig, 76
Black, Bud, 146
Black, Joe, 23, 42, 47, 55
Black Sox Scandal, 107
Blue, Vida, 58
Blyleven, Bert, 86
Boddicker, Mike, 55
Boggs, Wade, 61
Bonilla, Bobby, 9, 151
Boras, Scott, 114
Boston Beaneaters, 80
Boston Braves, 26, 42, 72, 84, 113
Boston Red Sox, 6, 12, 19, 26, 28, 33, 45, 54-55, 111, 129, 145, 149, 153
Boston Rustlers, 100
Bowa, Larry, 33

Branca, Ralph, 113
Braun, Ryan, 74-75, 126, 129
Braves Field, 109
Brett, George, 104, 110
Brock, Lou, 18, 132
Brooklyn Dodgers, 23, 26, 64, 84, 113, 124, 133, 136, 149
Brouthers, Dan, 15
Brown, Kevin, 151
Browning, Pete, 14-15
Bruton, Bill, 139
Buckner, Bill, 145
Burrell, Pat, 117
Burroughs, Jeff, 121
Bush, "Bullet" Joe, 153
Butler, Brett, 48
Cabrera, Miguel, 58, 136, 140-141
Caldwell, Ray, 138
California Angels, 93, 135
Callahan, Jimmy, 22
Caminiti, Ken, 12
Camnitz, Howie, 146
Campanella, Roy, 17, 45
Candaele, Casey, 12
Canseco, Jose, 73
Carbo, Bernie, 33, 129
Carey, Max, 100
Carolina Mudcats, 58, 141
Carpenter, Hick, 15
Castillo, Luis, 151
Cedeno, Cesar, 33
Cepeda, Orlando, 95-97, 99
Cepeda, Pedro "Perucho," 96
Chamberlain, Joba, 136, 139
Chambers, Al, 104
Chapman, Ray, 138
Charboneau, Joe, 20-21
Chesbro, Jack, 30
Chief Wahoo, 27
Chicago Cubs, 18, 42, 45, 72, 76, 95
Chicago White Sox, 13, 18, 22, 63, 68, 84, 89, 95, 106-107, 109

Chicago White Stockings, 80
Cincinnati Buckeyes, 26
Cincinnati Reds, 13, 23, 33, 72, 79, 95, 99, 118, 122, 129, 139, 147
Cincinnati Red Stockings, 126
Claire, Fred, 16
Clarke, Fred, 146
Clarkson, John, 80
Clemente, Roberto, 53
Cleveland Blues, 80
Cleveland, Grover, 100
Cleveland Indians, 10, 26-27, 38, 46, 63-64, 67-68, 84, 107, 138-139
Cleveland Naps, 10
Cleveland Spiders, 27, 32
Cleveland Municipal Stadium, 28
Cleveland Stadium, 20
Clines, Gene, 61
Clyde, David, 86, 117
Cobb, Ty, 6-7, 10, 30-31, 36
Cochrane, Mickey, 111
Colavito, Rocky, 28
Colorado Rockies, 54-55, 110, 126, 145
Columbia University, 96
Comiskey, Charles, 89
Comiskey Park, 20
Conigliaro, Tony, 33, 129
Conine, Jeff, 101, 141
Cora, Joey, 117
Corcoran, Larry, 80
Cox, Bobby, 148
Crandall, Del, 37, 69
Crenshaw (Ca.) High School, 122
Cronin, Joe, 72
Cuyler, Kiki, 100
Damn Yankees, 20, 143
Dark, Alvin, 26, 69
Davis, George, 32
Deadball Era, 22, 71, 138
DeBerry, Hank, 42
DeCinces, Doug, 135
Delahanty, Ed, 69

Derby, George, 80
DeShields, Delino, 16
Detroit Tigers, 7, 30, 34, 36, 38, 57, 64, 72, 83, 129, 146
Dickey, Bill, 45
DiMaggio, Joe, 6, 68, 104, 108-109, 115, 136, 154-155
Di Salvatore, Brian, 96
Doby, Larry, 84-85
Dodger Stadium, 63, 79
Douthit, Taylor, 147
Doyle, Brian, 143
Dressen, Charlie, 23, 133
Dropo, Walt, 68
Dunn, Jack, 111
Duren, Ryne, 55
Durocher, Leo, 113
East Cateret (N.C.) High School, 114
Easter, Luke, 46
Eastlake (Ca.) High School, 120
Ebbets, Charlie, 42
Ebbets Field, 23
Eldred, Cal, 78
Ellsbury, Jacoby, 144-145
Ennis, Del, 71
Erstad, Darin, 117
Essegian, Chuck, 149
Fain, Ferris, 63
Feller, Bill, 38
Feller, Bob, 6-7, 26, 28, 30, 38-39
Fenway Park, 26, 45, 61
Fernandez, Alex, 151
"Fernandomania," 7, 34, 48, 63
Fidrych, Mark, 6, 34, 56-58
Finch, Sidd, 41
Finigan, Jim, 91
Fisk, Carlton, 73, 129
Flaherty, John, 41
Flint (Mich.) Central High School, 93
Flintstones, The, 33
Florida Marlins, 58, 118, 120, 141, 151
Ford, Whitey, 7, 55, 145, 154-155
Foxx, Jimmie, 30, 36, 68
Francona, Terry, 145
Freeman, Buck, 67, 69
Garcia, Pedro, 101
Garciaparra, Nomar, 19
Gehrig, Lou, 68, 115
Gehringer, Charlie, 109
General Mills, 38
Georgia Tech, 19
Gettysburg (Pa.) Academy, 88
Gettysburg (Pa.) College, 88
Gibson, Bob, 34
Gibson, Josh, 46
Gilliam, Jim, 133, 149
Girardi, Joe, 127
Gomez, Ruben, 96
Gonzalez, Adrian, 120
Gooden, Dan, 34
Gooden, Dwight "Doc," 28, 34-35, 104
Gooden, Ella May, 34
Goodwin, Danny, 104, 117
Gott, Jim, 16
Grace, Mark, 120
Green, Ed, 64
Greenberg, Hank, 28
Greening, John, 64
Greenville News, The, 10
Griffey Jr., Ken, 57, 60-61, 121
Griffey, Sr., Ken, 60-61

Grim, Bob, 91
Groat, Dick, 23
Gromek, Steve, 84
Grove, Lefty, 111, 147
Guidry, Ron, 55
Gutierrez, Ricky, 76
Gwynn, Tony, 110, 120
Haddix, Harvey, 133
Hamilton, Josh, 118-119
Hardy, Joe, 20, 143
Harrist, Earl, 84
Harwell, Ernie, 57
Hazle, Bob "Hurricane," 136, 139
Helling, Rick, 143
Hernandez, Keith, 34
Hernandez, Livan, 7, 55, 150-151
Hernandez, Orlando, 151
Hillsborough (Fla.) High School, 34
Hobbs, Roy, 143
Homes (Miss.) Community College, 81
Hoffer, Bill, 80
Home Run Derby, 19, 118, 130
Homestead Grays, 46
Horner, Bob, 7, 83, 86-87
Hornsby, Rogers, 102
Hostetler, Chuck, 64
Houston Astros, 12, 33, 63, 76, 79, 81
Howard, Elston, 6-7, 44-45
Howser, Dick, 45
Hubbs, Ken, 101
Huizenga, Wayne, 151
Hurdle, Clint, 104, 110
Hutchinson, Fred, 13
International League, 45, 72, 111, 133
Jackson, Joe, 10-11, 102
Jackson, Reggie, 76, 79
Japanese Central League, 50
Japanese Pacific League, 53
Japanese Leagues, 48
Jefferies, Gregg, 104
Jeter, Derek, 7, 127, 143, 152
Jethroe, Sam, 26
Jobe, Frank, 16
"John Cosell Show," 25
Johnson, Darrell, 129
Johnson, Davey, 34
Johnson, Marques, 122
Johnson, Randy, 53
Johnson, Tim, 37
Johnson, Walter, 6, 30, 36, 104, 111
Jones, Andruw, 145, 148-149
Jones, Chipper, 6, 48, 106, 117, 121, 148
Jones, Ruppert, 101
Kaline, Al, 7, 83, 90-91
Kamm, Willie, 107
Kansas City Monarchs, 45, 124
Kansas City Royals, 51, 104, 110, 135
Karros, Eric, 17
Katalinas, Ed, 91
Keller, Charlie, 149
Killebrew, Harmon, 86
Kiner, Ralph, 67, 70-71
Kintetsu Buffaloes, 48
Kittle, Ron, 74
Knoblauch, Chuck, 152
Koch, Billy, 50
Koufax, Sandy, 28, 34
Kroc, Ray, 83
Kubek, Tony, 149
Lackey, John, 55, 146
LaMar, Chuck, 118

Langston, Mark, 69
La Russa, Tony, 9
Lasorda, Tommy, 17, 48, 63
Latimer, Scoop, 10
Lau, Charlie, 110
Lee, Derrek, 58
LeFlore, Ron, 18
Leifield, Lefty, 146
Lemon, Bob, 26
Ligtenberg, Kerry, 50
Listach, Pat, 74
Loiselle, Rich, 50
Longoria, Evan, 7, 130-131
Los Angeles Dodgers, 7, 16, 34, 41-42, 48, 55, 63, 79, 81, 95, 99, 121, 135, 149
Louisville Elipse, 15
Louisville Grays, 15
Lowell, Mike, 141
Lunte, Harry, 138
Lynn, Fred, 7, 124, 128-129
Lyons, Ted, 89
Maas, Kevin, 66-67, 143
"Maas tops," 67
Mack, Connie, 10, 46, 111
Maddon, Joe, 130
Maddox, Nick, 146
Maddux, Greg, 81
Mails, Duster, 138
Mantle, Mickey, 104, 115, 133, 148
Marquard, Rube, 107
Marichal, Juan, 58
Marion, Marty, 135
Maris, Roger, 73
Martin, Pepper, 7, 147
Martin (Tex.) High School, 106
Martinez, Pedro, 9, 16
Martinez, Ramon, 9, 16
Martinez, Sandy, 76
Mathews, Eddie, 23
Matsui, Hideki, 51, 101
Matsuzaka, Daisuke, 54-55
Mattingly, Don, 12, 67, 127
Mauch, Gene, 13, 76
Mauer, Joe, 117
May, Lee, 101
Mayberry, John, 110
Mays, Carl, 138
Mays, Willie, 6, 45, 69, 96, 112-113
McClymonds (Ca.) High School, 95
McCormick, Frank, 68, 109
McCovey, Willie, 13, 95, 98-99
McDonald's (restaurants), 83
McDougald, Gil, 28, 63, 133
McGee, Willie, 149
McGinnity, Joe, 46
McGraw, John, 46
McGwire, Mark, 67, 72-74, 95, 129
McInnis, Stuffy, 100
McKeon, Jack, 141
McQuillan, George, 22
McHale, John, 18
Meals, Jerry, 76
Melvin, Doug, 74
Meulens, Hensley "Bam-Bam," 67
Miami Dade Community College, 17
Microsoft Corp., 69
Miller, Rick, 129
Milwaukee Braves, 26, 99, 139
Milwaukee Brewers, 25, 37, 41, 74, 78, 126

Minnesota Twins, 14, 67, 69
Minnesota Vikings, 83
Minor League Player of the Year, 18
Minoso, Minnie, 57, 63, 95, 133
Monbouquette, Bill, 78
Montreal Expos, 16, 33-34, 76, 133
Montreal Royals, 124
Moore, Wilcy, 47
Morris, Jim, 7, 40-41
Morton, Carl, 33
Munson, Thurman, 79
Murakami, Masonori, 48
Murphy, Dale, 86, 117, 121
Murray, Eddie, 28, 101
Murtaugh, Danny, 96
Musial, Stan, 7, 136-137
My Turn at Bat, 26, 102
National League Championship Series (NLCS), 25, 141, 151
  1982, 25
  1997, 151
  2003, 141
NBA, 122
NBC, 38
National Association, 126
Natural, The, 143
Navarro, Lourdes, 117
Negro Leagues, 23, 26, 41, 45, 63-64, 84, 124, 133
Newark Eagles, 84
Newcombe, Don, 45
New York Giants, 42, 100, 107, 113, 115
New York Mets, 28, 34, 48, 58, 104, 122, 132
New York Times, The, 84, 109
New York Yankees, 23, 28, 42, 45, 47, 51, 53, 57, 63, 67, 79, 91, 109, 113-115, 127, 133, 138-139, 141, 143, 148-149, 152-153, 155
Nichols, Kid, 76, 80
Nomo, Hideo, 48-49, 58, 121
"Nomomania," 48
Oakland Athletics, 28, 72-73, 101, 106, 129
Oakland Coliseum, 28
O'Brien, Jack, 69
Oliva, Pedro, 14
Oliva, Tony, 14, 68
Olivo, Diomedes, 64
O'Neil, Buck 26, 45
Orie, Kevin, 76
Orix Blue Wave, 53
Ortiz, Ramon, 146
Oswalt, Roy, 81
Pacific Coast League, 22, 46, 72, 100, 107, 109, 138
Page, Mitchell, 28, 101
Paige, Satchel, 26, 57, 64-65
Palmeiro, Rafael, 120
Palmer, Jim, 57
Pedroia, Dustin, 7, 145
Pena, Carlos, 130
Pendleton, Terry, 121
Pennsylvania State University, 96
People magazine, 51
Pettitte, Andy, 53
Philadelphia Athletics, 10, 36, 63-64, 68, 88, 91, 111, 147, 153
Philadelphia Phillies, 13, 22, 33, 42, 71, 78, 91, 99-100, 148, 155

Piatt, Wiley, 80
Piazza, Mike, 17, 74
Piazza, Vincent, 17
Piniella, Lou, 50
Pinson, Vada, 13, 99
Pittsburgh Pirates, 22, 26, 28, 42,
    47, 64, 67, 86, 96, 100, 104, 146
Plain, Dealer (Cleveland), 20, 27
Plank, Eddie, 88
Pluto, Terry, 20
Pollet, Howie, 71
Polo Grounds, The, 42, 113, 153
Providence Grays, 96
Puckett, Kirby, 69
Pujols, Albert, 6-9, 68, 74, 81, 101
Quaid, Dennis, 41
Radatz, Dick, 78
Raines, Tim, 18
Rangers Ballpark in Arlington, 41
Raschi, Vic, 63
Ray, Johnny, 101
Reagan County (Texas) High School, 41
Reuss, Jerry, 63
Reyes, Anthony, 55
Reynolds, Allie, 23
Rhines, Billy, 80
Rice, Jim, 129
Richard, J.R., 34, 78
Rickey, Branch, 23, 26, 84, 104,
    124, 147
Rigney, Bill, 96
Ripken, Cal Jr., 117, 121, 126, 134-135
Rivera, Mariano, 139, 153
Rizzo, Johnny, 71
Roberts, Robin, 42, 99
Robinson, Frank, 13, 72-74, 94-95
Robinson, Jackie, 23, 26-27, 45, 84,
    124-125, 133
Rodriguez, Alex, 53, 74, 116-117, 121
Rodriguez, Francisco, 7, 147
Rodriguez, Victor, 117
Rogers, Steve, 78
Rookie, The (movie), 7, 41
Rookie of the Year, 9, 12-14, 16-20,
    23, 26, 28, 33-34, 42, 48, 50-51,
    53, 55, 58, 61, 63-64, 67, 69, 71,
    73-74, 76, 78, 81, 86, 91, 93,
    95-96, 99, 101, 113, 121-122,
    124, 126-127, 130, 132-133,
    135, 139, 145-146
Rookie of the Year Award, AL
    1951, 63, 133
    1955, 28
    1954, 91
    1962, 78
    1964, 14
    1977, 28, 101
    1980, 20
    1982, 135
    1984, 69
    1986, 73
    1987, 73
    1989, 61, 93
    1990, 67
    1992, 74
    1996, 127
    1997, 19
    2000, 50
    2001, 53
    2002, 146

    2003, 51
    2007, 145
    2008, 130
Rookie of the Year Award, Major League
    1947, 124
Rookie of the Year Award, NL
    1950, 26
    1951, 113, 133
    1952, 42
    1952, 23
    1956, 95
    1957, 139
    1958, 96
    1959, 13, 99
    1964, 13
    1967, 132
    1970, 33
    1978, 86
    1981, 18, 63
    1983, 122
    1984, 34
    1991, 12
    1993, 16-17
    1995, 48, 121
    1998, 76
    2001, 9, 81
    2003, 58
    2006, 55
    2007, 74, 126
Rose, Pete, 34
Rosen, Al, 46, 74
Roth, Braggo, 71
Rothschild, Larry, 41, 151
Rudi, Joe, 28
Russell, Reb, 22
Ruth, Babe, 46, 67, 104, 111, 115
Ryan, Nolan, 106
Safeco Field, 53
Sain, Johnny, 84
Saito, Takashi, 55
St. Louis Browns, 38, 104
St. Louis Cardinals, 9, 25, 91, 122,
    133, 135-136, 139, 146-147, 149
Salmon, Tim, 147
Sanders, Ben, 80
San Diego Padres, 83, 110, 120, 126
San Diego State University, 110
San Francisco Giants, 48, 79, 96,
    99, 147
San Francisco Seals, 107, 109
Sasaki, Kazuhiro, 50
Sauer, Hank, 42
Schuerholz, John, 110
Scioscia, Mike, 17, 63, 146
Score, Herb, 28-29, 34
Seattle Mariners, 50, 53, 61, 69,
    101, 117, 152
Seaver, Tom, 7, 124, 132
Seeley, Blossom, 107
Seibu Lions, 54
Sele, Aaron, 19
Sesame Street's "Big Bird," 57
Sewell, Joe, 136, 138
Shea, Frank, 55
Shea Stadium, 34
Sheffield, Gary, 141, 151
Simmons, Al, 72
Simms, Mike, 12
Sisler, George, 104-105
Slagle, Jimmy, 69

Slapnicka, Cy, 38
Slaughter, Enos, 136
Sledge, Terrmel, 120
Smalley, Will, 32
Smith, Ozzie, 86
Smith, Reggie, 149
Sockalexis, Louis, 27
Soriano, Alfonso, 152-153
Soto, Mario, 122
South Atlantic League, 30, 95
Southern Association, 42
Southern (Md.) High School, 91
Spahn, Warren, 113
Spencer, Shane, 136, 143
Sporting News, The, 28, 36, 64, 71, 78
Sports Illustrated, 20, 41, 57, 91,
    110, 143
Stengel, Casey, 115, 155
Strasburg, Stephen, 110
Strawberry, Darryl, 104, 122-123
Stuper, John, 24-25
Sudlersville (Md.) High School, 36
Sutter, Bruce, 18, 25
Sutton, Don, 63
Suzuki, Ichiro, 14, 52-53
Tampa Bay Devil Rays, 7, 41, 118
Tampa Bay Rays, 130
Taylor, Brien, 114
TBS, 117
Team USA, 93
Temple, Shirley, 38
Tenace, Gene, 148
Texas Rangers, 118, 120, 143
Thomson, Bobby, 113
Tiant, Luis, 48, 58
Tiger Stadium, 57, 129
Time magazine, 38
Texas-Oklahoma League, 22
Toronto Blue Jays, 101
Towers, Kevin, 110
Trosky, Hal, 68, 74, 109
Tulowitzki, Troy, 74, 126
Turner, Ted, 86
UCLA, 124
Union Club of Morrisania, 126
University of Alabama, 138
University of Miami, 17, 74
University of Michigan, 93, 104
University of Minnesota, 83
University of Notre Dame, 27
University of Southern California, 73
University of Texas, 106
Upper Deck Co., 61
Urbina, Ugueth, 120
Utah Stars, 83
Valentin, John, 19
Valentine, Ellis, 122
Valenzuela, Fernando, 7, 18, 34, 48,
    55, 58, 62-63
Vance, Dazzy, 42-43
Vanek, Ollie, 136
Van Meter (Iowa) High School, 38
Van Poppel, Todd, 106, 121
Veeck, Bill, 46, 63-64, 84
Vernon, Mickey, 46
Verstegen, Mark, 19
Waddell, Rube, 69, 107
Walk, Bob, 55
Waner, Lloyd, 133
Waner, Paul, 100

Ward, John Montgomery, 95-96
Washington Nationals, 64, 110
Washington Post, The, 36, 104
Washington Senators, 23, 36, 42, 69, 138
Washington Statesmen, 69
Watson, Bob, 12
Weaver, Earl, 101, 135
Welch, Bob, 76, 79
West, David, 104
Westminster Christian (Fla.) High, 117
Wilber, Del, 14
Wilhelm, Hoyt, 7, 23, 42
Williams, Jimmy, 68, 109
Williams, Jimy, 19
Williams, Marvin, 26
Williams, Ted, 17, 26, 33, 68, 102-103,
    122, 136
Williamson, Ned, 69
Willis, Dontrelle, 58-59, 141
Willis, Vic, 146
Wilson, Jim, 37
Wiltse, Snake, 88
Winfield, Dave, 7, 83
Wood, Kerry, 76-77
World Series, 7, 10, 25-26, 45, 47,
    55, 58, 63, 76, 79, 84, 118,
    120-121, 127, 130, 133, 138,
    145-147, 152-153, 155
    1909, 146
    1913, 153
    1918, 153
    1919, 10
    1920, 138
    1923, 153
    1927, 47
    1929, 111
    1930, 111, 147
    1931, 147
    1948, 26, 84
    1950, 155
    1951, 133
    1955, 45
    1975, 129
    1978, 76, 79
    1981, 7, 63
    1982, 25
    1995, 121
    1996, 127, 148
    1997, 58, 141, 151
    2001, 152-153
    2002, 146
    2003, 58, 118, 120, 141
    2004, 145
    2007, 55, 145
    2008, 130
Worrell, Todd, 50
Wright, George, 126
Wright, Harry, 126
Wright, Jaret, 55
Wrigley Field, 76
Yankee Stadium, 129, 143, 145, 155
Yale University, 25
Yastrzemski, Carl, 6
Yokohama BayStars, 55
Yomiuri Giants, 51
York, Rudy, 74
Young, Chris, 120
Young, Cy, 100
Yount, Robin, 7, 30, 37, 61
Zimmer, Don, 83

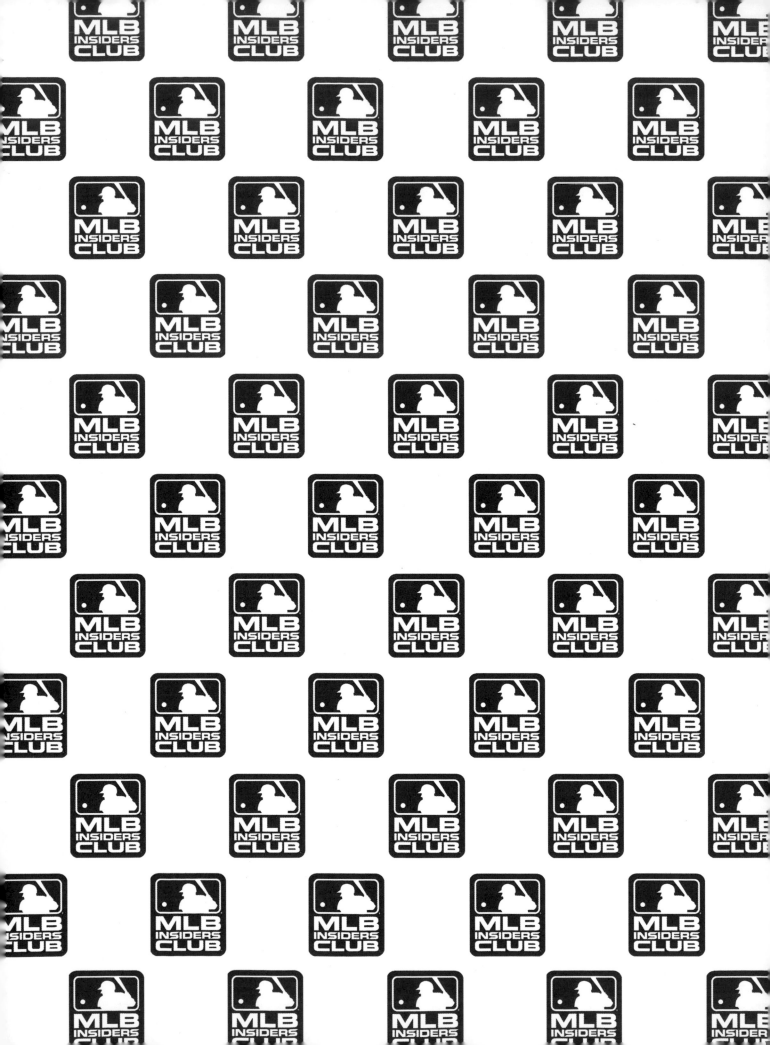